PN Review 247

VOLUME 45 NUMBER 5 MAY – JUNE 2019

REPORTS

POEMS & FEATURES

REVIEWS

SOME CONTRIBUTORS

Samira Negrouche was born in 1980 in Algiers where she still lives. She is a poet and translator, and doctor. Her books include: *A l'ombre de Grenade* (2003), *Le Jazz des oliviers* (2010) and *Six arbres de fortune autour de ma baignoire* (2017). Poems of hers, in Marilyn Hacker's translation, have appeared in journals including *Banipal*, *Pleiades*, *Words Without Borders*, *Modern Poetry in Translation* and *PN Review*. **Marilyn Hacker** is the author of fourteen books of poems, most recently *Blazons* (Carcanet 2019) as well as sixteen books of translation from French, including Vénus Khoury-Ghata's *A Handful of Blue Earth* (Liverpool, 2017). **Lisa Kelly** is chair of *Magma Poetry*. Her debut collection *A Map Towards Fluency* is forthcoming from Carcanet, in June 2019.

ON THE COVER: Alison Wilding, 'Drone', courtesy of the artist.

Editorial

ON APRIL FOOLS' DAY – the first day of National Poetry Month in the United States – the poet Jeremy Sigler published an interview with his friend 'the fearlessly outspoken critic and Stanford titan on the contemporary poetry canon, the complexities of O.J. Simpson, and the non-Zen of John Cage', better known as Professor Marjorie Perloff. The interview appeared in *Tablet Magazine: a new read on Jewish Life*.

Perloff has contributed essays to *PN Review*: on Tom Raworth most recently, and before that in 2013 'Towards a Conceptual Lyric' and, earlier, on 'Anna Akhmatova in Translation', on the Duncan/ Levertov correspondence. Her first contribution in 1981 was entitled 'One of the Two Poetries', a sustained response to *British Poetry since 1970*, a critical anthology I edited with Peter Jones. It was the beginning of an intermittent dialogue with Professor Perloff and other critics whose different points of view – because there is dialogue – illuminate the poetries they advocate and amend our own emphases, failures of contextual understanding and generosity. Her 1981 essay ends with praise for Christopher Middleton and 'the sense that our differences are not, after all, irreconcilable'. Of *PNR*'s hospitality, she remarks, 'Perhaps this is where Leavis's call for a "humane social order" comes in.'

She was fifty when she first wrote for us. Now she is in her eighties. She claims that, 'going back and rereading these old reviews after all these years', reviews published between 1969 and 2017 that constitute her two-volume retrospective *Circling the Canon*, due out in the autumn, 'I have to admit, I have hardly ever changed my mind'. What she has done is widened her circles and maintained a slant perspective on the scene and the canon. 'A number of my harsh reviews were of fellow critics, for example, Helen Vendler and Harold Bloom,' she admits. Her judgement has not changed, her understanding has. 'It's strange to read these reviews now, as I have come round to appreciating both of them much more. Both care so deeply about poetry, and this passion is ultimately what matters to me most.'

What she shies away from (and this makes her a distinctive voice at a time when gossip and appraisal often go hand in hand) is her distrust of biography. It can be

> very misleading. Roland Barthes was right in the early '60s to proclaim 'the death of the author'. All he really meant was that one cannot regard the work as just the materialization of aspects of the author's life, which was the standard academic mode of criticism in the various 'Life & Letters' series so common at the time. The work itself was seen as no more than an emanation of the life.

That prejudice insists that each genuine writer possesses, and must discover and develop, an individual 'voice', and the role of the critic, like that of a journalist, is to identify it. Yet how easily we are led astray by gossip and voice-hints. An example:

> My dear friend and major William Carlos Williams scholar Emily Mitchell Wallace believes that the suggestion, made by the various biographers, that Williams had many extramarital affairs, simply isn't true. She thinks the so-called evidence in the poems, which have such erotic moments, is largely a matter of fantasy.

It is refreshing when a critic restores the function of narrative to the work of art, and finds aesthetic rather than biographical reasons to validate a work. Perloff also knows that information and knowledge are not the same thing. We can recount the intimate and accidental facts of a writer's life but know little of the content and meaning of those facts. The witnesses themselves are not to be trusted:

> John Ashbery passed away recently and his biography is in the works. Karen Rothman, the author of Ashbery's biography (first volume published, the second to come), was in town recently and interviewed me. [...] I couldn't help thinking that biographers must be careful not to trust interviews too much because, after all, we who are interviewed don't quite tell the truth as we see it.

Perloff's career began with Yeats, Lowell and then Frank O'Hara. She reviewed his *Art Chronicles* in the *New Republic*. A publisher invited her to write a book on O'Hara. 'I didn't want to write a biography because I am not really a biographer. My O'Hara book is a critical introduction.' The publisher was disappointed with the first draft: 'they wanted me to bring in more biography. But I was reluctant because O'Hara's untimely death [...] had been the subject of much romanticizing and lurid speculation and I didn't want to get involved in all that.' The book is personal in an unusual way, one which connects with the critic's purpose:

> While I believe in being scholarly, I can't write the usual impersonal, even-handed academic text. I used to have colleagues [...] who would never ask themselves if they liked the books they taught: They just taught them. I find that impossible. I only teach what I love. I've taught modern poetry, and can't conceive of having to cover every 'leading' poet. I usually omit Robert Frost.

O'Hara opened into the avant-garde and Perloff has focused on writers who understand and then question convention. At a time when each new wave of prize-winning writers is enthusiastically applauded, her voice is perspectived and corrective. Her modernist avant-garde, now behind us, continues to defy. Perloff's interview begins, 'it's just not a great moment for poetry'. That's not what the competition judges say, their enthusiasm delivered in sound bites.

'I'm not eager to write poetry criticism right now,' Perloff adds, 'because the current scene strikes me as pretty unchallenging *vis-à-vis*, say, fiction or documentary.' Poets who seemed likely to make a difference have been sucked into the 'main stream', or come to terms with it:

Charles [Bernstein] and I have wonderful debates about what's happening in poetry. As a poet, he naturally wants to like a lot of work, but I find it difficult to agree. Look, when the language school of poetry started out, Charles was the radical, oppositional poet who brilliantly demolished 'Official Verse Culture', as he called it. But now, alas, much of what he previously condemned, like the 'transit theory of poetry—from me to you' has come back with a vengeance. Now the criterion for poetry is very romantic again, filled with the witnessing of personal pain and suffering, whether in relation to gender or race or disability, and so on.

It's a felt judgement: 'and so on' only just contains her impatience. She will not conduct a discussion of poetry and poetic theory in the unstable zones of contemporary civic correctness where expression is inhibited by a focus on the unidentified 'you' in the transit theory: 'your' assumed susceptibilities determine 'my' language.

By contrast, in her recent book *Edge of Irony* (2018), which attracted a substantial readership in Eastern Europe, Sigler notes, 'you point out how this diverse, multilingual, and vast geographical culture' – of Middle Europe – 'was shrunken into a nationalistic, predominantly conservative Germanic area of land, virtually overnight. You compare its diminished shape on the map to a tadpole.' Perloff distinguishes microaggression and macroaggression, and the way in which the first can morph into the other:

A microaggression is an unintended slight to someone who lacks your privilege, usually a member of a minority group. And such micro-aggression taps into deep-seated prejudices in our culture. But a macroaggression is not a question of insulting words but of overt and hurtful action against someone.

It was the latter which forced the Perloff family to emigrate from Vienna in the 1930s. Another species of microaggression has (temporarily, one hopes) helped to silence the 'Stanford titan on the contemporary poetry canon'.

Cover Story

Alison Wilding, 'Drone'

IN THE ART OF ALISON WILDING, motifs are often chosen in order to be rendered minimal, subjected to a semiabstracting process that turns the object into a powerfully encrypted meditation on the emergence of form and the disclosure of an idea. It is therefore unsurprising that she should have become fascinated by constructions designed to be secretive about themselves. Stealth bombers and drones in particular have elicited her sustained attention: both attempt to withdraw from the visible signs of the world, to create an effect of dematerialisation, to deny the force of gravity. Wilding's art is about shape-shifting. She has observed in conversation, 'I see the drone as a contemporary malignant sprite not unlike Ariel in Shakespeare's *Tempest.* I am drawn to the conflicting spectacle of beauty/speed/devastation in all its manifestations.' The drone embodies the spell of a mechanical efficiency that cloaks its deadly potential. So much of Wilding's work is about encryption and concealment – the implying of what is hidden. For her, the perception of meaning must always combine looking with sensing – the visible with the virtual image.

ROD MENGHAM

News & Notes

Poetry trafficking in Colombia · A poet in Usaquén, to the north of Bogotá, was arrested on 10 March for selling poems in the street during an artisanal festival. The martyr to verse is Jesús Espicasa. He had set up a stall where, on an old manual typewriter, he was composing poems in return for a donation. Espicasa was declared to have 'invaded public space' and asked to move on. He refused, the police were called, and the poet was carted off and fined the equivalent to $260 dollars, the largest fine allowable under the police code. That's a lot for poetry. Asked what his crime was, the police spokesman replied, 'trafficker in poems'. The police offered no samples of the offending produce.

A Continent of Poetry · Brunel University's seventh annual International African Poetry Award, worth £3,000, announced its shortlist at the end of March. African poets from around the world who have yet to publish a full collection are eligible. Each poet submits ten poems to a panel of judges, this year including three poets – Matthew Shenoda (Egypt), Leila Chatti (Tunisia) and Phillippa Yaa de Villiers (South Africa). More than a thousand entires were reduced to ten finalists, the winner to be announced on 30 May:

Afua Ansong (Ghana)
Mary-Alice Daniel (Nigeria)
Inua Ellams (Nigeria)
K. Eltinae (Nubian Sudan)

Omotara James (Nigeria)
Selina Nwulu (Nigeria)
Jamila Osman (Somalia)
Nadra Mabrouk (Egypt)
Emmanuel Oppong (Ghana)
Sherry Shenoda (Egypt)

Previous winners include Warsan Shire (Somalia), Romeo Oriogun (Nigeria) and Theresa Lola (Nigeria). 'When I started the prize in 2012, African poetry was almost invisible on the literary landscape. Today there are legions of poets out there successfully building careers and being heard,' declared Professor Bernardine Evaristo, Professor of Creative Writing at Brunel.

Turning a century · Lawrence Ferlinghetti has lived to see the counter-culture institutionalised. He turned a hundred on 24 March. He is, one critic said, 'a living monument', which is better than being a dead one. 'The Beat poets began the counterculture movement in the arts; that is the reason all the artists I know are still here in San Francisco,' Andrew Sean Greer, a San Francisco-based novelist who won the 2018 Pulitzer Prize for *Less*, declared in an eloquent celebratory non-sequitur. 'Ferlinghetti and his friends changed the city from men in gray flannel suits to poets in leaky basements, black and female and queer poets even then,' Greer told CNN. 'We're a continuation of that hope and rage and art. I still go to Caffe Trieste with a friend to write and Vesuvio to drink and City Lights for poetry.' San Francisco celebrated its surviving Beat. City Lights Bookshop hosted an 'open house', art galleries featured Ferlinghetti's photos and paintings. The Mayor declared 24 March Lawrence Ferlinghetti Day. There were celebrations in New York (he was a child of Bronxville). 'He is so very beloved by his friends and neighbours in North Beach and people all round the world,' the punk art surrealist Winston Smith, who designed the controversial Dead Kennedys' album cover, *In God We Trust, Inc.*, in 1981, said. 'Putting up with the human race for a full century deserves a reward,' he added.

One reward has been book sales. *A Coney Island of the Mind* with over a million copies in print – translated into over a dozen languages – has outsold even Rupi Kaur. It is, Amiri Baraka declared, 'one of the banners of an emerging generation's quest to remake American poetry'. Neruda told him in 1960 in Havana, 'I love your wide-open poetry'. For Robert Creeley he is 'our determined conscience, our wit and eloquence – our steadfast friend and witness – and our communal wisdom's articulate, patiently old-time voice. Would that all might stand as he and be counted.'

A New Divan: A Lyrical Dialogue between East & West · To honour Goethe and the 200th anniversary of the first publication of the *West-Eastern Divan*, his great poem sequence of 1819, *A New Divan – A Lyrical Dialogue between East & West* presents twenty-four outstanding new poems by leading world poets, with facing English-language versions by leading contemporary poets, to create a conversation between languages and cultures. Two of the poems are featured in this issue of *PN Review*. 'This reimagining of Goethe's seminal work gives us the opportunity to re-engage with his thoughts – a much needed exercise, given the state of the world today,' writes Daniel Barenboim in his Foreword.

The poets come from across the East – Morocco to Turkey, Syria to Afghanistan – and from across the West – Germany to the United States, Estonia to Brazil. Writing in Arabic, Persian and Turkish, and English, French, German, Italian, Portuguese, Russian, Spanish and Slovenian, each pair of poets has responded to one of the themes of the twelve books of Goethe's original *Divan*, including 'The Poet', 'Love', 'The Tyrant', 'Faith' and 'Paradise'. Working with the original poems or by bridge translations, the English-language poets create new poems that draw on the poetic forms and cultures of the poets taking part. Three pairs of essays accompany the poems, mirroring Goethe's original 'Notes and Essays for a Better Understanding of the *West-Eastern Divan*'. Bill Swainson and Barbara Schwepcke brought the book together. 'The "Gingko Biloba" was Goethe's ode to friendship,' writes Schwepcke, 'and symbolised the union between old and young, man and woman, human and the Divine, literature and scholarship, East and West – a union which in [Goethe's] mind was inseparable.'

Rotterdam jubilee · This year's Rotterdam Poetry International Festival celebrates its fiftieth anniversary, from 13 through 16 June in De Doelen, Rotterdam. All the international poets participating in the festival will take part in the opening event. The line-up includes Rita Dove (United States), Kayo Chingonyi (Zambia/UK), Mona Kareem (Kuwait), Antjie Krog (South Africa), Lieke Marsman (Netherlands), Patricia Lockwood (United States), Koleka Putuma (South Africa), Vahni Capildeo (Trinidad/UK), Charles Bernstein (United States) and Raúl Zurita (Chile). The full festival program will soon appear on line.

What survives · The award-winning American poet Linda Gregg died in March at the age of seventy-six. Emily Langer commented on her life and work. 'Gregg was nearly 40 when her first book of poetry, *Too Bright to See*, was published in 1981. She followed it with half a dozen more volumes, attracting praise from poets as distinguished as the late W.S. Merwin, who lauded her poems as "original in the way that really matters. They speak clearly of their source," Merwin observed in comments published by the Poetry Foundation. "They are inseparable from the surprising, unrolling, eventful, pure current of their language, and they convey at once the pain of individual loss, a steady and utterly personal radiance."' In 'Lies and Longing', she described a scene in a women's homeless shelter:

> Half the women are asleep on the floor
> on pieces of cardboard...
> An old woman sings an Italian song in English
> and says she wants her name in lights:
> Faye Runaway...
> One keeps talking about how fat she is
> so nobody will know she's pregnant.

In 'Wrapping Stones' her austere, thrifty style approaches personal revelation:

> Everything I am is what survived
> love's leaving. Everything I see, eat, want,
> have is what survived the goneness

of what love is. Love, like time, takes down
the house, leaving only the partial walls,
open squares of light for windows,
and a door.

She insisted, 'Certainly one can make good poems without feeling much or discovering anything new. You can produce fine poems without believing anything, but it corrodes the spirit and eventually rots the seed-corn of the heart.'

Much ado about very little · On 27 March the Associated Press announced that the grave of Anne Bradstreet, the first published American poet, was once again being sought: 'professors and students at Merrimack College in Massachusetts are trying to pinpoint her burial site while at the same time restoring her legacy and what they say is her rightful place in the pantheon of Western literature.' 'Even though we don't know much about her, she was a household name in the seventeenth century, both here and in England,' an assistant professor of English at Merrimack announced, a little implausibly. The best that can be said is that she was not unknown, which is not quite the same thing as being a household name. Two associate professors 'are leading several students in the project, dubbed Finding Anne Bradstreet'. The poet is believed to be buried somewhere on the Merrimack campus. 'The aim is to use ground-penetrating radar to find subterranean disturbances that might indicate a burial site. Given the passage of time, there are unlikely to be any remains, and even if there are, there are no plans to exhume them.' One student declared, 'I just thought finding the grave of America's first poet sounded exciting and very Indiana Jonesy.' But without a shovel.

No mention of John Berryman's 'Homage to Mistress Bradstreet', the poem in which she genuinely survives.

Spoken jazz · Richard Sandomir remembers the poet Ken Nodine, who died in February at the age of ninety-eight. He 'improvised poetry in a silky voice to cool, vibrant musical accompaniment, creating a form of storytelling that he called 'word jazz', and that brought him renown on radio and led to collaborations with Fred Astaire, Tom Waits, Jerry Garcia of the Grateful Dead and other artists. [... He]

> became wealthy doing voice-overs for television and radio commercials. But he found his passion in using his dramatic baritone to riff surreally on colors, time, spiders, bullfighting, outer space and dozens of other subjects. His free-form poems could be cerebral or humorous, absurd or enigmatic, and were heard on the radio and captured on records, one of which earned a Grammy nomination.

'I like jazz,' he said, 'for the principle of what jazz is: a flight of musical fantasy within structure. [...] I'm trying to do the same thing verbally: take off on a theme so you become tangential and transcendent at the same time.'

From the Archive

Issue 147, September–October 2002

SINÉAD MORRISEY

From the poem 'The State of the Prisons: A history of John Howard, Prison Reformer, 1726–90'. Fellow contributors to this issue include Carola Luther, R.F. Langley, Marilyn Hacker, Jeremy Over, Geoffrey Hill and John Ashbery.

from THE STATE OF THE PRISONS

I am a stranger and a pilgrim here.
I burn my letters, decline a monument, take heart
from the body's incontinence. The spirit departs.
The field hospitals of Russia with their horrendous dead
must carry me home to the Lord my Maker
where all my fathers' fathers stand assembled.

I see these soldiers' faces when I sleep.
And then they cloud and clear again as the child's
who stopped me on the road to ask the time
and tried to steal my watch. How sick she is.
And then she splits, becomes three women beating hemp
in a bridewell, missing eyelids.

Death has no terrors for me.
I have ridden the devil's coach-road, I have discovered
it leads, in every city in Europe, to the mansions of governors...
Powders fizz in a glass. The admiral who has travelled
thirty miles to smile encouragingly
tries to change the subject but his voice unravels.

[...]

Diving into What Wreck?

Part I

VAHNI CAPILDEO

The first time I read Adrienne Rich's *Diving into the Wreck* was probably in the 1990s or early 2000s, during the course of a relationship so quietly abusive that I may never write about it directly. I envy the mythmaking ability, or the clarity, of people who can remember poetic 'first times': their first encounter with a word, 'gnu' or 'yeast' or 'scintillating' or 'quotidian', their first encounter with an author, or indeed with poetry. I cannot vouch for the memory of 'first times'; only fought-over or pirated intervals, within which always-explosive limits it became vaguely or fiercely possible to do things alone. In any case, to the reader I then was, *Diving into the Wreck* seemed new. I had not realised that the publication date was the same as the year of my birth, and that its stripe of feminism had stayed news in the course of my individual life, and the countless other grab-and-run-reader lives resembling mine. Re-reading is a quick way to feel older; especially when what drives the reader back to a foremother's poem is the need to set it alongside astonishing long poems by one's own younger contemporaries, such as Sumita Chakraborty and Gail McConnell – more of that in the next magazine, as this is Part I of II.

Staying with the earlier point, for a moment: what is an 'older' reading – perhaps one that is more crowded, and more volatile? Perhaps one that is more self-aware? I wish that critics, and 'ordinary' poetry readers, were trained in self-questioning their unconscious world-building as second nature, just as Londoners mostly learn to 'mind the gap' and not fall onto the tracks in the Underground, or as I learnt not to put my feet or hands unthinkingly into heaps of leaves or holes in rocks or trees, in snaky Trinidad. Here in Part I, the memoir of reading is not so that 'you' can learn about 'me', and what strange ideas I had. It is an invitation to jump into your own wreck, and to retrospection.

Looking at Rich's opening stanza –

> First having read the book of myths,
> and loaded the camera,
> and checked the edge of the knife-blade,
> I put on
> the body-armor of black rubber
> the absurd flippers
> the grave and awkward mask.
> I am having to do this
> not like Cousteau with his
> assiduous team
> aboard the sun-flooded schooner
> but here alone.

– it occurs to me that the sea setting would have given me the confidence to slip easily into this poem from the outset, as if into a non-alien, non-alienating context. Now I reflect that her dive may have been intended to be heroic, the shipboard liminal, the environment unsettling. I taste the cynicism of her first line: yeah, guys, I've done my homework (and your canons of taste are a pack of lies). Then, it had lacked startlement: it harmonised too much with the archipelagic Caribbean poetry and the Latin and Greek translated lore of my childhood, which were part of my imagination's deep structure. Any sea was the Atlantic Ocean and so in any sea-words I, we, could be at home. Into Rich's feminist, allegorical, North American water, I painted a blend of warm and cold currents, turquoises and scarlets, fire coral and angel fish, drowned guns and dangling gold. Is reading partly a site-specific practice? Should it, could it, court dissonance, and become both more and less so? What might a Home Counties reader find if they delved similarly into their first, or early, *imaginings around the reading of* poems from the Orkneys, Belfast, Guyana, Vancouver, Tamil Nadu?

Rich's dismissal of Cousteau and crew did not register as a rejection of masculine power, fame and authority. Because her dismissive lines made way for a 'sun-flooded schooner', I felt as if Kamau Brathwaite and Derek Walcott were within friendly signalling distance, I did not call their names in a marginal note; I could not have put this entirely misleading feeling of neighbourliness into words. As for 'black rubber' and 'the grave and awkward mask', and the altered pace that comes with the absence of commas. Here, surely, were vengeful and godly Carnival spirits, and here even more surely was not BDSM, with its home cinema of consensual hurts, but the world-stage domesticity of abusive relationships between nations, the half-concealed and outrageous truth of the global north-sponsored assassination and undermining of revolutionaries and reformers.

Rather than decoding Adrienne Rich's text, I naïvely encoded it as not cold, as not reducible to code, as belonging to belonging. Is this kind of waywardness and self-deception, or reading-into, the way that people do 'enjoy' poetry, before having to ask themselves hard questions about what they assume to be the poem's 'place'? (Is this a necessary illusion and sympathy, before (self-)questioning and empathy kick in?) Is a feeling of ease the readerly equivalent of falling for 'false friends' in translation – two words with similar roots but divergent meanings, so that the careful 'fastidious' in English becomes the tiresome and pernickety 'fastidioso' in Spanish? Is the opposite reaction – a feeling of exclusion, unfamiliarity – a hint that it is the reader who may need to reset their compass, not the poem?

By stanza 8, Rich's speaker has dived into the wreck. The word 'wreck' occurs for the fourth time in the body of the poem. As an 'older' reader, I am struck not only by the insistence on disaster, and salvage, but by the implicit opposition between 'wreck' and 'craft'. Rich is insisting that what survives of the tradition, what she can access as a maker, is sunken and requires extraordinary efforts. Her craft is not something she captains, or that surges along with admiring or fabulous creatures in its wake. By implication, and by repetition of 'wreck', the notion and word of 'craft' itself is not so much sunken as thoroughly boarded and bombed into absence. I am also struck by how blasé my younger, briny self was to the presence of wrecks, literally understood despite being symbolically intended – the sea as the biggest postcolonial war grave – how blasé I was about the impulse to plunge, or plunder. What else could the task be except retrieval from ruins, probably illegitimate, unlicensed, untelevised? Well, I was at the wrong intersection. Rich's poem is after gender:

This is the place.
And I am here, the mermaid whose dark hair
streams black, the merman in his armored body.
We circle silently
about the wreck
we dive into the hold.
I am she: I am he

A description of the merman follows the stanza break, but there is a deliberate pause at 'I am she: I am he'. Again, what the poem may have deployed as radical seemed perfectly normal; I was then unaware that in some Afro-Caribbean religions, people of any gender can be ridden by gods of any sex, but there was a sense of it in the culture, and my own religion featured the discus-twirling warrior god Vishnu's female avatar, Mohini, her photocopied hourglass form featuring in helpful educational charts alongside a variety of more warlike incarnations (men and beasts). I wonder now if this stanza implies a feminist critique of profound psychic wounding, a polarisation into binary gender roles, a splitting of the poetic self that even undersea is forced to inhabit some kind of male body in order to go places. However, what I took from it was the more radical ability to be plural. Plurality, metamorphosis, marvel – the powers of poetry – will be explored in Part II, in close readings of Chakraborty and McConnell, in whose books of myths more names do appear.

Yangon, City of Tolerance

JAMES JENNINGS

Tolerance is not a word you would immediately associate with today's Myanmar. The 2017 Rohingya killings shocked the world. The outlook for this new democracy remains deeply discouraging. While opinion-makers continue to conjecture about the true motivations of the government, the one thing everybody here agrees on about the National League for Democracy is its incompetence.

Living in the capital, Yangon, the news can be disheartening. What is to be done? I have found that one of the best tonics to ward off the despondency is a stroll around the old city, which seems to tell a happier story about people's ability to put up with each other.

Still known to many as Rangoon, the city of Yangon does not reveal its charms easily. I have been here for over five years, yet I cannot say I know it well. It is certainly not an easy place to live. After all, the British built it in a swamp, their only interest being the adjacent river, which was suitable for a port. After its trading heyday, Rangoon was hit hard by World War II, and then even harder by bad government. In 1942 the Japanese began their *blitzkrieg*, and two decades later General Ne Win seized power. Rangoon went into long-term decline. Nowadays the city is still in a state of decay, despite some efforts to polish the place up. Edifices that the British Raj bequeathed to Burma skulk like half-sunken battleships, and blots of mould blacken the tightly packed buildings.

In other words, we are not working on very promising beginnings. And yet, Rangoon, Yangon, has the power to seduce. It rains a lot here. The last monsoon was as torrential as any. Wherever you look, lush foliage bursts from antiquated guttering; leaves wave merrily from drenched plaster facades. Trees don't just grow around the houses, but from them. Most modern cities make some kind of pact with nature, creating parks and gardens within planned spaces. But unlike nearby Bangkok, for example, a shiny metropolis drowned in ferro-concrete, the organic bond with the forest was never severed in Yangon. The battle against nature was lost before it started. The jungle is still there, along with the great expanse of water, as Pablo Neruda observed in 'Rangoon 1927' (in Alastair Reid's translation):

a city
of blood,
dreams and gold,
a river that flowed
from the savage jungle
into the stifling city
and its leprous streets

That cramping sense of closeness to the natural world is still there, and it may help to explain why the old city is such a tolerant place. In this tight urban knot, where gargantuan tree roots pulverise the foundations of decaying residences, civility is not a choice but a survival tactic. The rain that leaks into my neighbour's house is the same rain as drips into mine.

The central hub of the Buddhist metropolis is the Sule Pagoda, two-and-a-half millennia old. What is fascinating about Sule is not its age, but how Hindu and Muslim temples coexist happily within a few hundred yards of the great Buddhist shrine.

The people who came to Burma in the eighteenth and nineteenth centuries were responsible for much of this plurality. In many respects, at the dawn of the twentieth, Rangoon was an Indian town, but it was also peopled by immigrants from further afield – Persia, Mesopotamia, Afghanistan. Sucked in by new opportunities offered by the Empire, families set themselves up as traders, bankers, shopkeepers and clerks. The ordinary Burmese became decorative features of the colonial backdrop. Small wonder they felt resentment.

A few steps west along Mahabandoola Road is the Cholia Jamah Mosque, where the Tamil-speaking Muslims worship. Just to the left down 29th Street is the astonishing Jain Temple, in which a polished teak staircase leads to a splendid upper room with chequered tiles and altars carved in white Indian marble. One block along, 30th Street boasts the Mogul Mosque, the home of the small Shia Muslim community, which arrived from Persia and beyond, as the family names carved in the forecourt make clear: Sherazee, Ispahany, Kabuli. At the corner of Bo Soon Pat Street is the dolls' house-like Shri Satyanarayan Temple, where two time-blackened silver doors conceal the gold statues of Vishnu and Lakshmi. A few minutes away, the Jewish faith has its synagogue in 26th Street, guarded by a Muslim porter. Burma's Jewish families were from Baghdad, and the elegant, crumbling Sofaer mansion, built by the dynasty of the same name, was once the finest department store of the Far East. Ten minutes' walk away, down by the container port, is the exquisite temple which the Chinese migrants from Hokkien built to the sea goddess Mazu, in gratitude for having reached Burma's shores alive. The list goes on. Those willing to brave the heat and walk up to 40th street will find the oldest Christian church in Yangon, the Armenian Apostolic Church of St John the Baptist.

Other cities have their temples where different faiths come and worship. There is nothing new about that. What makes Yangon so special is the sheer proximity of these religious places. There is a promiscuous good neighbourliness to this fecund, crumbling city in which pluralism thrives. Discord is rare. Of course, this damp little acre is a very different world to the horrors of northern Rakhine State. We must pray that it endures.

Jonas Mekas Recalled

CHRISTINE BLACKWELL

Jonas Mekas, widely known as 'the godfather of avant-garde cinema' and largely credited with developing diaristic filmmaking, passed away in New York last January at the age of ninety-six. During his lifetime he not only witnessed firsthand at least four avant-garde art and literary movements in formation (the Beat generation, Pop Art, Fluxus, post-modernism), he also befriended and participated alongside several of the artists in each, filming everyday moments of their lives as well as of his own. His films employed chance and thus lacked plot or linear narrative, yet they were lyrical and captured fleeting moments of joy and beauty just as they became memory.

Mekas left a huge cultural legacy as a filmmaker but also as a critic, organiser, poet and perhaps most importantly, as a friend to and protector of avant-garde artists. In 2010 he said:

> The avant-garde is always the front line in any field. That's where it's all very fragile, and on the front line is where usually most of the bullets hit... It's that area that I felt needed somebody who would defend it from all those critics and those attacks. So that was my function, to try to help those very fragile new developments.

In 1954 he founded the influential journal *Film Culture.* Then from 1958–75 he served as film critic for *The Village Voice*. All the while, he continued making his own films, notably *Walden* and *Lost, Lost, Lost*. His contributions also included the co-founding of the Film-Maker's Cooperative and the Filmmakers' Cinematheque (1970) in New York. Initiated in the early 1960s, the Cooperative gave other experimental filmmakers a place to share and discuss their films, as well as get their movies distributed when no commercial distributor would touch them. Out of financial necessity, Mekas first ran the Cooperative from his Manhattan loft. It was here that he began to meet other avant-garde thinkers including Salvador Dali, Allen Ginsberg and Andy Warhol. Later, John Lennon and Yoko Ono also moved into his sphere. The Filmmakers' Cinematheque, which is now called Anthology Film Archives, is considered one of the world's premiere archives and museums of avant-garde film.

All the while he was filming and writing about films, Mekas was writing poetry. In fact, poetry had been his main creative outlet in Lithuania before his emigration to the US in 1949 as a displaced person who had spent several years before in a German labour camp. His poems about his life as a young man in Lithuania are now considered classics in his country of birth, and over the course of his life he published more than twenty books of verse and prose.

So how did this seemingly tireless, ageless wonder manage to accomplish so much in one lifetime? He always claimed that he would remain twenty-seven his entire life, the age he was when he arrived in New York City and to a second chance. And it looked as though he managed that feat, at least internally. I met with Mekas on several occasions when he was in his eighties, and he indeed appeared youthful despite his wrinkles. The first time we talked, I was with my friend Billie Maciunas, poet and widow of George Maciunas, 'chairman of Fluxus'. Fluxus at the time was becoming (and is still becoming) recognised as a fully-fledged international art movement. We had gathered in Cipriani restaurant in New York while we awaited a gallery owner to discuss Fluxus artwork. I knew that Mekas had been best friends with George Maciunas, a fellow LithuanianAmerican, and he had participated in Fluxus activities himself, but that was all that I knew. However, I was surprised when this slim octogenarian wearing a floppy fedora and loose suit jacket hoisted a video camera onto his shoulder and started filming. Then the gallery owner arrived. After a few moments of chit-chat, the gallery owner attempted to negotiate a low-ball monetary deal for the Fluxus artworks still under Billie's control. I knew then why Mekas was really there; it was as protector and friend, not only of Billie, but of his old friend George Maciunas and the legacy of Fluxus. Needless to say, it was Mekas, already with years of experience protecting avant-garde artists, who stopped the deal. Billie remained in control of her legacy.

In 2010, Mekas organised a wonderful book launch at the Emily Harvey Foundation gallery for *The Eve of Fluxus*, the flux memoir by Billie Maciunas. And quite an eve it was, with prominent writers, artists and filmmakers, as well as art historians from around the country, joining in to celebrate. And, of course, Jonas Mekas was there, too, clearly celebrating, but also watching, sometimes from the wings.

from The Notebooks of Arcangelo Riffis

Marius Kociejowski

Arcangelo, when we last saw him, was standing behind the reception desk of a small hotel in Nevern Square, the pages of his manuscript scattered like a gaggle of frightened geese, a look of surprise in his face, no time to think, no time even to take a swing at me. That single action of mine, my throwing his verses in his face, would interrupt our relationship for close to two years. I'd got him dead centre. I'd rocked his pride. America had just pulled out of Vietnam. Some hullabaloo, Uncle Sam on the run, desperate Vietnamese clinging to the skids of fleeing helicopters.* *Operation Frequent Wind.* Who was the poetical genius behind that verbal soufflé? A couple of weeks before that first break in our friendship, Arcangelo and I watched the TV together in silence, in the hotel lobby where often I'd meet up with him late at night for talk – *talk* when things were 'good' between us or, when not, when words failed, renewed hostilities. This occasion was marked by a solemn truce. Saigon, April 29th, 1975. One of the men hanging onto the skids fell. It was no great distance. The desperation, on the other hand, the depth though which people who have lost their pride plunge, was immeasurable. We could applaud the *fact* maybe, the end of a foolish escapade, but not the bleeding shame of it all. There was something else, however, that Arcangelo did not dare give utterance to, which curled up inside him like burning paper, flaking off at the edges. It would be some years before I discovered what it was.

Shame. Maybe Arcangelo was the last of the human race to feel it, in its true classical sense. Shame, honour. Those are not words you can say now without an accompaniment of cackles. They were the north and south of his existence. They were his *Rome*. America would not let go of him nor could he let go of it and never more so than on the night we watched the sordid end of one of its worst ever debacles. America would come up at least several times in any conversation with him and try as I might to steer the course the country would continue to smoulder in his discourse. It got so I wanted to scream at the very mention of the place. This story is not, it will not be, I keep saying to myself, about America even if at every turn it insists on showing its face; it is about how one addresses, and is addressed by, the dead. But then a fellow writer slaps me down. 'Arcangelo without America,' he says, 'would be like Noël Coward without London.' Yes, I tell him, but this is not a battle I can afford to lose. All will be tarred with the same brush otherwise. Arcangelo's mistake was to resort to stereotypes. It was always the beastly and never the thoughtful American who entered his discourse. I argued with him, saying it was the worst blunder any poet could make, that the specific must be the goal if one's intention is to reveal the bigger picture. Arcangelo's failure to do so contributed to his poetic silence. I'm convinced of this. I couldn't shift him, though, for he was a metaphysical boulder of granite. We had come from opposite ends of the universe and Earls Court, London SW5 was our spreading galaxy's precise centre. We were bound to collide. Our skirmishes ever on the increase, it was time for one us to evacuate the bombed-out scene. I quit in a full blaze of fire or, rather, a scattering of pages.

A bad peace, says Tacitus, is worse than war.

I saw him twice during that time. The first was in winter of 1975, on a bitterly cold day. I'd surprised him in a back street not far from Earls Court Road and there he glowered at me as if cornered in some corner of his own making, clearly mortified, nostrils flaring like a horse's, sweating profusely in sub-zero temperature. Our conversation was awkward but polite. I suggested he visit some time and he balked at the absurdity of such a notion. Arcangelo wore his Prussian blue windcheater, 1950s vintage. A winter coat he would have deemed unmanly, something only for softies. It was the garment he wore when I first met him, it had already been through quite a few seasons, and it was the garment that thirty-four years later still hung from the door of the room where he died. Because he'd spent the greater part of fifteen years in his room it was now crusty with age. It appears in his notebooks as I knew it would: *The Fairway 500 by Central of Boston*. A man wholly indifferent to appearances will go to extraordinary lengths to make sure he preserves that indifference and in so doing creates for himself an image he'd sooner die for than lose. Narrow though Arcangelo's world was, surely not more than five degrees on the compass, he was incredibly fussy, almost fetishistic, on the matter of his dress, to the extent that the clothes he sought were the clothes that were no longer made. They were decidedly square although once upon a time they might have issued straight out of *Rebel without a Cause*. 'You want my jacket,' says Jim Stark to a shivering Plato, 'it's warm.' Plato declines. It's the single, most tender, moment in the movie.

A few months before he died, Arcangelo, much to my surprise, watched *Brokeback Mountain* and remarked on how moved he was by the final scene when, in an act of remembrance, the character of Ennis Del Mar takes a clothes hanger and gently places his checked cowboy shirt over the blue denim shirt of his beloved and dead friend, Jack Twist. It was, in its way, a brave film although certain things in it did not ring true. Would those two men have so recklessly, so passionately and so publicly kissed in the street of a small town at *that* time, in the 1950s, when such things were so hidden as to be incomprehensible? It struck a false note. Those very shirts recently sold for $100,110.51 and now hang in the home of the late western movie star, Gary Cooper. I don't know who bought them. Arcangelo, who abhorred not 'flits' but rather what they did in private, could comprehend the manly love between men. That final scene in the movie, which might equally have been Achilles mourning the death of Patroclus, epitomised for him all that was allowable between males. The tenderness with which Arcangelo writes about men is only rarely matched by what he writes about women. There is, in the latter, almost always a snarl-up of some kind.

Snarl-up, his phrase.

* It was one of Arcangelo's many verbal tics that he'd always refer to them as 'heliocopters'.

Letter from Norfolk

Mocking February

MARTIN CASELEY

The song of the lawnmower is again heard throughout the land, as the weather continues to confound expectations. This time a year ago, the Beast from the East snowed us all in; now, we bask (according to the Met Office) in a West African plume of heat. 'A calm of pleasure listens round / And almost whispers winter bye', says John Clare, in 'February' in *The Shepherd's Calendar*.

This is good, because that other far-off scratching sound is the political war of attrition continuing, igniting hidden seams of anger all round. The smoke rising from this battlefield threatens to choke all rational debate. Cycling the lanes is one way of escaping the Babel of raised voices. After nearly a week of record temperatures and sunny afternoons, the trees are exhaling. Crops look complacent in the fields and the hedges flaunt glossy ivy.

Streams run and ponds stand, but the old tag of 'February fill-dyke' seems wildly inappropriate. When I lived in Worcestershire, B.W. Leader's Victorian landscape of the same name often seemed to illustrate the watery ditches and footpaths: damp cottages and rutted gateways were the order of the day, but now there are calm, dry lanes at lunchtime and dust rises in the wake of Land Rovers as they crunch past.

February, like November, seems a familiar Victorian vista in poems and paintings. Alice Meynell's poem 'In February', to take a generic example, hymns a 'colourless sky of folded showers' only for its prophetic power when it is related to the coming spring. Elemental energy and signs of new life are only latent. It is the 'miles and miles of unsprung wheat' that excite thoughts of what waits 'beyond the portal', an interesting charged moment of delayed gratification. Larkin found a similar image for potentiality with the 'postal districts packed like squares of wheat' in the great cumulative momentum at the end of 'The Whitsun Weddings'. The rest of the colouring in the Meynell poem, however, blears the picture into stasis and conventionality: beneath her sky lies only the 'grey morn'.

Leader's palette in his great painting is more dramatic: watery skies shimmer in puddles, the cloudscape seems to include livid greys and purples, but is anchored by shades of brown and green in the waterlogged field. Critical journals in 1881 found something thoroughly English in this. Unlike Meynell's poem, nothing is held back; it is not a sentimental view fit for a Victorian cottage wall – you would get pretty muddy if you tried to walk through the landscape depicted. Rows of fleecy clouds at the very top of the painting suggest a mackerel sky, scales that may presage a change of weather. It doesn't see the month as a kind of prelude to spring – it aims for veracity, even though, according to some accounts of the painting's genesis, it may actually be based on a November evening.

This portentous, shape-shifting uncertainty is part of February's charm. We don't quite believe the warm weather and feel duped, somehow: this isn't what we were braced for. Still, the sparrows float across lanes and scrap in hedges as if summer's already here; pheasants perform their Road Runner strut across the traffic, bereft of roadsense; cats laze on warm bins. The lanes grow fringes of shadow and prospecting crows flap lazily away across the fields, but it could all be a trick: Clare, ever alert for signs, called it 'mocking weather' and it feels suitably unreal.

IN FEBRUARY
Alice Meynell

Rich meanings of the prophet-Spring adorn,
Unseen, this colourless sky of folded showers,
And folded winds; no blossom in the bowers;
A poet's face asleep in this grey morn.
Now in the midst of the old world forlorn
A mystic child is set in these still hours.
I keep this time, even before the flowers,
Sacred to all the young and the unborn.

To all the miles and miles of unsprung wheat,
And to the Spring waiting beyond the portal,
And to the future of my own young art,
And, among all these things, to you, my sweet,
My friend, to your calm face and the immortal
Child tarrying all your life-time in your heart.

Vintages

PATRICK WORSNIP

Castel del Piano, Italy – all is forgiven now. Well, more or less. A mere seven centuries after the city of Florence, birthplace of the poet Dante Alighieri, drove him into permanent exile, things are much more relaxed these days between the descendants of the man who wrote *The Divine Comedy* and those of his fourteenth-century enemies.

We may think divisions over Europe have got nasty again in recent years. But anyone who's read the *Comedy* will know that feelings ran even higher in medieval Italy, especially in Tuscany between the Guelph and Ghibelline factions, who (to summarise crudely) respectively favoured the Pope and the Germany-based Holy Roman Emperor in the struggle for control of the continent. In Florence, the Guelphs were dominant, but they themselves were split into the Whites (to whom Dante belonged and who tended towards the Ghibelline position) and the Blacks. In late 1301, while the poet was on a mission to the Holy See in Rome, the Blacks seized power and persecuted prominent Whites. Dante was accused of corruption during a brief stint as a city official, a crime known at the time as 'barratry', meaning the sale of Church or state favours. This is punished in the poet's *Inferno* by the offender being dunked in boiling pitch, but the punishment Dante himself received on the doubtless trumped-up charge was two years' exile and a large fine. When he refused to pay up, the exile became permanent and he was threatened with death if he ever went back to his native city. He never did, spending the rest of his life moving around various cities including Verona, Sarzana on the Ligurian coast and, finally, Ravenna on the Adriatic, where he died, possibly of malaria, in 1321, aged fifty-six. He was buried there in a Roman sarcophagus next to the St Francis basilica. A Latin inscription on the tomb by his friend Bernardo Canaccio brands Florence a 'mother of little love'. The poet himself had already lashed back at the city, crowing in the bitterly sarcastic opening to Canto 26 of the *Inferno* about the number of Florentines he had placed there:

> Florence, rejoice – you're such a mighty town,
> you flap your wings across the land and sea;
> the whole of Hell is filled with your renown!

Broadly aware of these details since embarking on a *terza rima* translation of Dante's fourteen-thousand-line masterpiece, I became much more interested after visiting a medieval festival a year or two ago in the Umbrian town of Gubbio, not far from where I spend my summers. There I attended a meeting which the organisers, with that Italian flair for the theatrical, staged between a direct descendant of Dante, Count Sperello di Serego Alighieri, and Antoine de Gabrielli, descended from Cante Gabrielli, who, though a native of Gubbio, was the *Podestà* (mayor) of Florence who pronounced Dante's sentence in 1302. (Antoine's family moved to France centuries ago and he is a French businessman living in Paris.) The meeting was all embraces and *bonhomie*. Among other things, Sperello recounted how the Alighieri name nearly died out in the sixteenth century, when it looked likely to terminate with a female descendant of the poet called Ginevra. She married a certain Marcantonio Serego and they had a son, Pieralvise. The name was saved when his heirless great-uncle stipulated in his will that the boy must add his mother's surname, Alighieri, to his father's. Since then, the problem has not recurred.

Before too long after Dante's passing, Florence decided that, if it had not wanted him alive, it was more than happy to have him dead. It made repeated requests to Ravenna to send the body, all of them rejected. After Pope Leo X authorised the move in 1519, a delegation from the Tuscan city went to collect the sarcophagus, but the custodians had managed to hide the poet's remains in a false wall and the Florentines went home empty handed. In 1829, an ornate tomb was built for Dante in the Santa Croce basilica in Florence. It has stayed empty to this day and he is still in Ravenna.

In the twentieth century, efforts got under way to clear Dante of the charges of which he had been found guilty. In 1966, a year after the 700th anniversary of his birth, a mock retrial was held – but, significantly, in Arezzo, one of many Tuscan cities with which Florence was at loggerheads in the Middle Ages (Arezzo was Ghibelline). The participants – jurists and historians – included Giovanni Leone, later to become President of Italy, in the role of one of the judges. In a concluding verdict, the 'court' stated that it 'unanimously declares the supreme Dante Alighieri not guilty and acquits him'.

Finally, in 2008, the Florence city council approved, by nineteen votes to five, a motion brought by centre-right councillors that revoked the sentence passed seven hundred and six years earlier. Communist and Green councillors, however, labelled the move a 'stunt' and said that, had Dante not been exiled, he might never have composed one of the greatest works of world literature. 'If he'd been condemned to death, would we have been asked to resurrect him?' joked one Communist councillor. Sperello's cousin Pieralvise, a wine-grower near Verona, refused to attend a planned ceremony to receive, as a symbol of reconciliation, a gold florin from the city whose bankers had once built its wealth on the coin. Citing comments by the opponents, he explained in an interview with the *Corriere della Sera* daily that he had decided to pull out because of 'petty polemics'. 'When I read about the council session I realised it wouldn't be a heartfelt, collective "mea culpa" at all,' he said. 'My heart sank when I read certain remarks.' The newspaper commented: 'It's as if the citizens of Stratford-on-Avon were squabbling over an event commemorating Shakespeare.' And I was saying about Guelphs and Ghibellines?

Following the Gubbio event, I resolve during my next stay in Italy to meet with Sperello, having discovered that he lives – conveniently for me – in Umbria. He agrees readily enough and invites me to call on him at his family home south-west of Perugia. This turns out to be the Villa Aureli, a fine eighteenth-century residence in the otherwise undistinguished little town of Castel del Piano. Within seconds of my ringing at the gate facing onto the road, five dogs come bounding out, barking furiously, followed by their owner, who assures me: 'They're good-natured.'

The clothes Sperello is wearing on this warm, sunny morning, a scruffy T-shirt and shorts, do not exactly match the luxurious long gown I've seen in many an illustration from Dante's period. But he himself, it strikes me, bears a strong physical resemblance – despite the passage of twenty-one generations – to the poet, in particular the chiselled profile with its long, pointed nose. I point this out tactfully, but he says: 'It's a coincidence.'

Sperello brings out coffee and we chat at a table in the extensive manicured gardens of the villa, surrounded by lime trees, fruiting lemon bushes and neatly clipped box hedges, and overlooking an unblemished landscape of rolling hills. The gardener, Raffaele, potters in the background. It may not be quite the earthly paradise where Dante, in his vision (for want of a better word), arrives after being guided through Hell and Purgatory by the Roman poet Virgil, and where he waits to be accompanied to the heavenly Paradise by his beloved Beatrice. But it's idyllic enough. The villa was constructed in its present form by Count Sperello Aureli (to whom my host owes his unusual first name) and passed to the Alighieri family through marriage in 1918. Sperello's father, Leonardo, made it his main residence and spent much of his life restoring it. Sperello defrays maintenance costs by renting out an apartment in it with original eighteenth-century furniture and frescoes.

We talk about the long-running feud with Florence. Sperello made a conciliatory gesture in 2015 by attending celebrations there in Santa Croce of the 750th anniversary of Dante's birth. He found himself next to mayor Dario Nardella (who, renewing the tradition of out-of-town mayors, is Neapolitan by birth). 'Nardella shook my hand and said the city of Florence apologises,' Sperello says.

'After so many centuries, it's not a problem.'

Indeed, Sperello (who retired shortly after we met) made the latter part of his working life in Florence, commuting from Castel del Piano to spend weekdays there. As it happens, he is an astrophysicist by profession – a noteworthy fact given that the structure of the heavens is central to the *Paradiso*, the third part of Dante's poem – and worked at an observatory in the hills just outside the city. Prior to that, he worked for the European Space Agency (ESA) in the Netherlands and Germany and was later director of a centre for the Italian Galileo telescope on the Canary Island of La Palma. An important part of his career has involved enabling the ESA to collaborate with the American-built Hubble Space Telescope. And while he may not have matched Dante's travels through Hell and Heaven, he did once ride his motorbike from Italy to Beijing.

With all this in mind, I ask the inevitable question about what it feels like to be a descendant of Italy's greatest poet. 'It's not my fault,' he smiles. 'I wanted to do my own thing. I wanted to be appreciated for who I was. But now I've thought about it again. I read Dante at school, like everybody, but it didn't interest me much – I was an astrophysicist. But ten years ago I got interested in Dante's astronomy. For Dante, astronomy was very important.' Although the poet believed in the pre-Galileo earth-centred Ptolemaic system, 'he does say that a galaxy is made of lots of stars. He realised he was at a moment when things were changing.'

Sperello also became interested in the 'two cultures' problem and says that Dante's era spelled the end of the polymath. 'After Dante it wasn't possible to know everything. I don't even know everything about astronomy. We have to try to communicate about science and meet people in other fields.' At the same time, he says he is a religious believer, having been brought up in a religious family, and does not see science and religion as fatally contradictory, despite differences in approach.

One lesson Sperello has learnt from his illustrious forebear was inscribed on a bookmark his father gave him in his childhood. Taken from the opening lines of Canto 16 of the *Paradiso*, it concerns the vanity of a famous name unless descendants constantly buttress it through achievements of their own:

> Nobility of blood, how scant you are...
> You are a cloak that quickly shrinks; each day
> new fabric must be stitched on, otherwise
> time's scissors go round snipping it away.

Now, in an Italian play on words, he says he sees inheriting the poet's legacy as simultaneously an honour (*onore*) and a burden (*onere*).

If Sperello has sought to live up to Dante's reputation through astrophysics, the probably better known branch of the Alighieri family is headed by his cousin Pieralvise, already mentioned, who makes wine in the Valpolicella area near Verona. And if that place name makes you think of boxed plonk you may have drunk at student parties back in the day, forget it – we are talking quality stuff here. This being Italy, the family wine business goes back to the Middle Ages. During his exile, Dante twice lived in Verona as guest of the local della Scala potentates. His family stayed on there and in 1353 his son Pietro bought vineyards in Valpolicella, which have continued to produce wine since then. The estate has served as the main centre of the Serego Alighieri family, which was reduced to one male descendant with Sperello's and Pieralvise's grandfather, also called Pieralvise. He had five children, however, and there are currently male heirs to carry on the name.

The leading vintage of the estate is a rich red Amarone. It's pricy and Sperello doesn't have any. Instead he offers me a bottle of red wine from his own vines in Umbria. I decide to keep it alongside a bottle of white I previously acquired from the descendants of Italy's second greatest poet Giacomo Leopardi, also counts, who make wine in the eastern region of Marche. Sperello reminds me that not everything in Italy lasts for seven centuries. 'Best drink it within a year,' he says.

Letter from Wales

SAM ADAMS

Because we have friends there, and commitments of one kind and another, we are often on the road that skirts Cwmbran ('valley of the crow' – a local stream) and Pontypŵl ('bridge of the pool') and rises sharply towards Penperlleni ('hill orchards'), one of the many entrances to rural Gwent, and heads northwards still to Abergavenny ('mouth of the river Fenni' – that is, its confluence with the Usk). As you approach the old market town, if it is a bright, clear day, though you have done this a hundred times before, you marvel at its setting. On three sides it is enclosed by mountains: to your left the Blorenge (the name of uncertain origin, but one of those rare rhymes with 'orange') at 559m., to the right the rugged and broken-backed Ysgyryd Fawr ('great split') at 486m, and straight ahead, dominating the scene, a symmetrical simulacrum of an extinct volcano, the 590m Sugar Loaf. They are not high, compared with the Black Mountains, of which they are the outliers, still less with the Brecon Beacons a little further to the north and west (some might think of them as hills), but as a backdrop to the town they are spectacular. You have a short while to enjoy the scene before the road bends and dips into Llanofer ('church of Myfor'), and the mind, pondering time-wrought transformations in place names as all else, turns from topographical to historical considerations.

English made early inroads into Gwent, the fate of a borderland, but it was not a steadily advancing linguistic tide. When industrialisation brought an influx of Welsh from the west and the north, the Gwent valleys became for a while a powerhouse of Welsh-language publishing and Welsh chapels flourished. And then there were individuals who devoted much of their lives to stemming the tide, by propagating Welsh language and cultural aims, some of whom had English family origins. Among the latter was a most remarkable woman – Lady Llanover. Augusta, youngest daughter of Benjamin and Georgina

Waddington, was born at Tŷ Uchaf ('upper house'), Llanofer, in 1802. Her family had come from Nottingham in 1792. In 1823 she married Benjamin Hall (1802–67). Her husband was third in a line of Benjamin Halls, a family originating in Pembrokeshire. His grandfather was dean of Llandaff cathedral, his father, a barrister, had the enormous good fortune to marry Charlotte, daughter of Richard Crawshay, the Cyfarthfa (Merthyr Tydfil) iron-master, who had come penniless out of Yorkshire and by luck (again a very advantageous marriage), hard work and an instinct for business, created an empire. In 1803, he was able to make Benjamin père a partner in the Rhymni ironworks, and in 1808 presented him with the 3000 acre Abercarn estate, neighbour to the Waddington's Llanover estate. This second Benjamin Hall, I have read, was known as 'slender Ben' on account of his delicate physique. It was not an indication of good health and, having attained a measure of fame as the first industrialist/politician in Wales, he died at the age of thirty-nine. His son, Augusta's husband, also became an MP, in 1831. He was created baronet in 1838 and in 1855 appointed commissioner for works. In the latter capacity he oversaw the construction of the clock tower at Westminster. He is said to have been a large man, well over six feet, and for this reason (underlining the contrast with his father) known as 'Big Ben'. It sounds to me a tall tale, but is nevertheless held to account for the familiar name of the clock tower and its chimes. In 1859, he became a peer, as baron Llanover of Llanover and Abercarn. His steady ascent to the peerage in turn explains why his wife is sometimes referred to as Lady Hall, though more frequently as Lady Llanover.

The devotion to the cause of the Welsh language and Welsh cultural traditions at Llanover is generally thought to begin and flourish under the influence of the mistress of the house, but in his sphere her husband was her equal. A strong advocate of Anglican church services in Welsh for Welsh-speaking congregations, he was active in the Disestablishment movement, which brought about the Welsh Church Act in 1914 and led in 1920 to the creation of a separate province within the Anglican Communion and the election of an Archbishop of Wales. He is remembered also for his battle in parliament against the iniquities of the 'truck system', by which employees in ironworks and mines were paid in tokens redeemable only in company stores – the cause of much unrest in industrial south Wales.

If the genesis of Lady Llanover's commitment to Wales, its language and traditions, can be pinned to any single event, it would be her attendance at a meeting of *Cymreigyddion y Fenni* (the Abergavenny Welsh Society), which was addressed by Rev. Thomas Price, vicar of Cwmdu in Breconshire. Known by his bardic name 'Carnhuanawc', he was a writer, an antiquary and an inspirational speaker. He did much to build relations between Wales and Brittany, not least by assisting the translation of the Bible into Breton, a language he had learned. He founded a Welsh school in his parish and, like Benjamin Hall, advocated services in Welsh and an end to the practice of appointing non-Welsh speakers to livings and bishoprics in Wales. This was a time when intellectuals elsewhere in Europe (though not in England) took a keen interest in Wales, its history and language. One among them,

Baron Christian von Bunsen, Prussian envoy to the court of Queen Victoria, married Lady Hall's older sister, Frances, and attended eisteddfodau at Abergavenny. At an eisteddfod in Cardiff in 1834, Lady Hall won a prize for an essay on the Welsh language. 'Gwenynen Gwent' (Bee of Gwent), her *ffugenw* (nom-de-plume) on this occasion stuck, for the good reason that it conveyed the extraordinary busyness of her life on behalf of Wales. She had the will (and the wealth) to promote her interests in the playing of the triple harp, in Welsh music and dance generally, in traditionally patterned Welsh cloth and costume – her servants at Llanover Hall wore the traditional costume of their counties of origin. As patron of the Welsh Manuscripts Society she stimulated the rescue and publication of ancient texts; she purchased the precious collection of Iolo Morganwg now in the National Library of Wales.

It is less widely known that she was instrumental in organising the writing – it is now thought by Jane Williams ('Ysgafell') – and publication of *Artegall*, a thirty-two-page pamphlet named after the knight of Justice in Spencer's *Faerie Queene*, as a response to *Brad y Llyfrau Gleision* (the *Treachery of the Blue Books*). It was printed in Llandovery by William Rees. Early in my research on Prichard, almost fifty years ago, I came across a series of letters to Rees in the Tonn collection at Cardiff Library. They were written from 'Llanover' and signed 'A.H.' – Augusta Hall. In one she says 'if Welsh men do not show a little courage, and self-respect now they deserve what they will otherwise have, the contempt of Europe'. Her anger is almost palpable in the vigour of her hand, and we can be sure that whoever wrote *Artegall*, it was A.H. who saw it through the press and arranged publication in London by Longman & Co. Looking over the pamphlet now (as you can do online) you can judge how effectively this rapier picked apart such argument as there was in the three volumes of the 1847 report of the inquiry into the state of education in Wales.

Language of the Day

From the Journals, 23 November 2001

R.F. LANGLEY

The language of the day again is birds. The cat's cradle handed us is again the estuary, the wide sky over it, the winter reedbeds. Some anticipated variations play out of this... the kingfisher on the pools in the reeds by the path beyond the wrecked rowing boat and the car tyre that have been there in the weaving for many years. There it goes, the turquoise brighter than anything expected in the rest of the scene, the vermillion right in with it, clashing, harsh richness, tiny detonation prolonged in the low dash over the biscuit-coloured reeds, their soft brown heads. The tide out, the mud wet and reflecting. Redshank beaks lowered to peck their own inverted tips. Curlews lifting and folding their feet as they step forward on the stickiness, treading on their inverted images, adhering to them. A stretched-out flock of dozens of dunlin, pale-stomached, grey-backed, along the reefs, with the redshank. Formations of flocks in the air as entities rippling and twisting. A lone hawk, white-breasted, dark-backed, very upright on a stump, then dashing low over the runnels, setting up the waders. The twanging of bearded tits by the hide, and I step to the door and here they are, barred in the reedstems, then clean on the rail of the walkway, rich chestnut, white, black, grey, sudden, seen or more, then gone again.

B returns with a viper draped over a stick, a thin dribble of blood along its lip, black eye, pale ochre, near cream, and the broken zig down it, the tail-tip still curling and stretching. Avocet, just a few, very pied in flight, extending their landing legs.

The potential of the given vocabulary is exciting, of course, of course, of course. We take it as a matter of course. The known population. The loud shelducks, brash, with bloodiest bills. The tits grabbing their way through the dense stems, jumping clear, whirring away, their calls a plucking sound with a wiriness in it, suited to snaps on verticals, to catching and loosing at once.

Colder today. Rain last night. Leave the dead snake in the soaked reeds and grass, chilled through, never a mammal, fish-like, eel-like, scaled, pale-stomached.

Inside, Blythburgh is tall, warmer than reeds, controlling the light, holding it on brick and matt stone. The Christmas cards cost nearly a pound each. Our black car is sprinkled with thin mud. Our kitchen is draughty – the wind blows round the light bulbs set into their holes in the lobby ceiling and in round the back door.

I clean our boots with the broom kept outside by the dustbin, poking the mud out of the grooves in the soles with the stiffest stems of dead herbs I can find in the bed there.

Charles shouts about the weather... how warm it still is, how we might pay for this later. Richard Johnson is in his jeep in the track, I can see him glance our way through the chopped hedge... but he doesn't speak and drives away, moments later, having checked his post from the box he has set up, having rejected having his letters in a plastic bag tied to the front fence. Darkening by half-past three. Warmest upstairs in the bedroom.

The language of birds and stems, and air movements and colour, here for some more interlacings. Sad. Sad means satisfied, sated, steadfast, full. Tipped off by the best touches, the kingfisher, flying garishness, gare, gag, to bend the head backwards – Norwegian... snap your head up into the stare, the staring colour, the jerk it gives as you catch it, stop, raise your head, gauren, to stare. 'Down from the castel cometh ther many a wight / To gauren on this ship and on Custance' (Chaucer, 'The Man of Lawe's Tale', line 912). Stare, inflexible, fixed look, firm, staring hair in a fright.

On then, a sad stare today, especially at the dead snake, his fixed eye, like a metal pellet, iron shot, in the limp body, under the little protruding eyebrow, along the long lips rimmed with blood. A staring day, the sun behind us, B stepping through the reeds with the viper draped on a stick, fetched from the wood where she went while I stayed in the hide. The language talks on. Richard's glance through the hedge, read from the twist of his peaked white cap. The lift of my head as the kingfisher glances. The flop of the viper's head, dropping its still glaring eye. That suddenness of seeing. B stepping round the reeds. The story of the Dawn Man from *Ages and Ages Ago*. 'The sun was sinking. Through a tangle of tall grass and trees a little man came stepping.' Carrying a stick. Watching out. Vulnerable. The opposite of the party in *The Lost World*, their first day of exploration, having seen the iguanodon and about to see the pterodactyls. 'At every second step, one or other of our professors would fall, with a cry of wonder, before some flower or insect which presented him with a new type.' Which sentence has almost as long a history in my mind. Two ways of proceeding, the one... 'As he walked, he shot quick glances about him, for in those times, there was danger everywhere', and the cries of wonder as you fall on the flowers. Staring. I know the two ways well enough. There is a blank second in both when it could be either. The jerk as the head goes up. The new thing. The difference in the deal. The gleek. To gaure at. To gare at. To gape, to pry, to gaw at something. That moment of stupid surprise. Set at the gaze.

edited by Barbara Langley, March 2019

The Moselle

Passages from the *Mosella* of Ausonius (fourth century A.D.)

ALEX WONG

Greenest of creatures,
up your left and right
Ridges garnished aromatically
With vines;
coated along the slopes
Of tender sides with turfy reaches;—

Ship-bearing as seas,
but sliding river-like
With a declining run; in lucid volume
Rivalrous with broad, capacious lakes;

Peer to rills and becks
in excitation; smart
Challenger to any chilly spring
For a pure cup;
little runnel,
Gush of the fountain:
what does either claim?—

Rivers, lakes, and the two-way refluent sea,
Ebbing and flooding: has any any merit
Wanting in you?

*

You prosecute a most unruffled lapse:
Singular, placid course. No mumble of wind
Furrows your top; rocks offer no vexation;

Burbling shallows never jostle you by
In tearing urgency; no islands jut
Obtrusive in the middle of your level:

A blemish on your name if any crag
Rose to divide and check your going,
Bother your bearing, its
mobile repose.

*

I can see you, sometimes,
checking yourself out:
How you admire
your own recursive passage,
Seeming often as though you thought
Its proper flow, its glide,
too slow, too idle, almost.

Grown in slime, ungainly sedge
Is not allowed to lace
your banks; you never spill
To either side, in the fashion of lazier rivers,
Sludgy frontiers:
cleanly go down the steps
That lead to your edge.

*

Let those who lack
Imagination

Pay for conspicuous
Pavements of
Mosaic—lay out
Expansive floors

Of lucent marble
In panelled halls.

For me (with a little
Sneer at what can be had for a stupid price),

I shall devote my admiration
To the present specimen of Nature's work,
Far from the nauseous bodings that annoy
People of prodigal taste;

But where an exuberant poverty
Wantonises, happy in its free,
Ever-renewed expense.

Here, solid sands invest the humid shores:
The press of approaching soles
Leaves no lasting figure to record them.

*

Through your smooth back
Your deep, pellucid spaces

(River keeping no secrets)
can be seen.

Now the delicate air
Relaxes, clear and easy:
Well-contented breezes
Stir no barrier through the vacancy:

With vision reaching down to intimate parts,
We make out solid bodies sunk.
Your innermost retreats
Float visible,
the waters going softly—
Flow with merest liquid
showing in tinted light
Scattering images,
diffusive forms:

The way the wrinkled sand
          is raked by the nimble currents;

The way the nodding grasses
Shudder tenderly,
Down in your greeny basement.

The driven weeds, beneath
          their own indigenous wave
Suffer continually its vibrancy.

*

Pebbles glance in the light
          and go to ground again.
The sand is shifting and sifting,
          the green moss peeping.

Wide Caledonian shores lie bared
To British eyes,
When fleeing tides
Leave the dark seaweed naked in the day,

And the pink corals and candescent pearls
(Oysters' seeds), delights of finders and buyers;
Lapping under well-stored waves,
Illusive jewellery mocks our human vogues:

As plainly as that,
          down in the blithe Moselle
Herbs of no single tone
          veil and denude
The little stones mixed up among their roots.

*

Well, there's something to look at,
          free to eyes that look:

The glaucous river redisplays
The massed opacity of hills,

So it seems the slipping waters go
Bosky with adopted leaves;
As if the sprigs
          of shooting vines
Grew in the river.
                    . . . The colour on its shine:—
When Venus comes, compelling shadows of night,
And splashes out the greenery
Of mirrored hills over Moselle.—

          The hunching summits
          Swim there whole,
          In curling quivers;

Distant branches eddy there: the clusters
Fatten across the face of a polished wave.

The boatman feels the trick: eyes down,
As, one by one,
                    slip under them   the tendrils
Stiffened with sap: he floats

          Alone in the tree-bark vessel
          Far out in the water

Where the copied hill confounds itself with the river,
And the river fits itself
          with the limits of the shadows.

*

When the bare sun floods down
With all a sun-god's heat,
He spills in the glassy course

The shapes of boys aboard their boats:
Wriggling forms of bodies upside-down.

As they repeat their stroke to left and right,
Throwing their weight to alternating oars,
The river renders   watery counterfeits
Of corresponding souls.
The boys take pleasure in their duplicates,
Lured by the fallacies the river returns.

So, before showing off
          her well-adjusted hair,
When grown-ups   for the first time
Prop up   for a little girl
The widely-shining,
          deep-inquiring mirror,
And gladly she discovers a novel game,
Seeing, she feels,
          a real, a sisterly face:

On gleaming metal, gives
          her unrequited kisses:
Fumbles there to affix
          her own deflected pins,
And catches at that brow,—
And means to run her hands in the dark curls;

Likewise, they, on their boats,
Drawn by these teasing idols,
Savour the figures, false and doubtfully true.

*

The wet catch dances on the arid rocks,
Quakes at the lethal missiles
Of the sunlight-bearing day.

Under its native waters, it knew strength.
Sapped in our atmosphere,
Life weakens in the element it gasps.

The invalid body pulses now
With indolent palpitations, torpid tail
Suffering terminal tremors, and the lips
No longer meet:
          the fish expels
The air it takes   by yawning gills,
Rejecting in breath what brings it to this death.

Reminds me of bellows, when they blow
To nourish workers' fires,

And the woollen valve cavorts in the chamber of beech,
And its blinking aperture sucks in, by turns,
And hinders there the wind it snatches.

I have seen fish convulse
Under the closing pressure of death, collect
Their spirit, hurl themselves into mid-air,
To give their tumbling bodies headlong back
To the river beneath,
Possessing again
The waters of which they almost had despaired.

*

The Sura—no
low-born degenerate,
Itself enlarged
by the bulk of two other streams—
Hurries to slip beneath your waves
And gratify you with its sum
of intercepted waters:

Nobler involved in you, become Moselle,
Than if it poured back to parental Sea
A negligible mouth.

Tributaries race
To reach your side, to lick
Softly against you their
submissive waters:

Rapid Celbis, known for its fish;
Erubris, rolling stones of mills
With flying revolutions in the corn,
And forcing strident saws
through blocks of luminous marble,
Hearing continual noise from either bank.

I have nothing to say about the lank Lesura,
Nothing about the tenuous Drahonus.
What can I do with Salmona's beggarly dribble?

Saravus, floating ships
on its wave-resounding mass,
Has been for some time in my sights
With all the draperies of its robe out loose,
Long drawing out its stream, so it might devolve
Its tired limits into you, beneath
The walls of Imperial Trier;
and Alisontia slides
Lightly, through the fields of fattening regions,
Skimming the fruitful lips of its domain.

A thousand others—each in the urge
Of its own persistent and peculiar impulse—
Want to be yours: the end of their ambition,
The satisfaction of their inborn humour;
These impatient streams.

Joseph Brodsky in Leningrad

PATRICK MILES

I ARRIVED IN MOSCOW on 10 September 1969 for a ten-month academic visit. I was twenty-one and as well as improving my Russian I wanted to see as much of the country and its people as possible, immerse myself in its nineteenth-century literature, and experience the Soviet poetry scene, which was widely thought to be the most vibrant in Europe.

In fact, this phenomenon was petering out. Although I had been enthusiastic about Yevtushenko's verse (particularly his love lyrics) as a teenager, by 1969 I regarded him as hopelessly compromised and had no desire either to hear him or meet him. Andrei Voznesensky was the most popular Soviet poet. I was mad about his love diary *Oza* (we were all in love with love in the 1960s), but I found his public reading bogus. When I met him and tried to discuss with him why he had not been let out for the recent Poetry International in London, I sensed an adept of the Soviet artistic elite. Some other poets were excellent (Akhmadulina, Okudzhava, Martynov), but none of them set me alight. There was always an elephant in the room: the genocidal system that had killed Gumilev, Yesenin, Mayakovsky, Mandelstam, Tsvetaeva before them. It was clear that this subject was unmentionable, as were almost the very names Mandelstam and Tsvetaeva. Moreover, in Moscow it proved impossible to get hold of new poetry in *samizdat*.

By Christmas 1969 I was thoroughly disillusioned with the Soviet poetry scene. I also needed a break from Moscow's claustrophobia. The standard cure was to apply for a study trip to Leningrad, which I did for the New Year. At this point I remembered reading the previous summer a selection of Joseph Brodsky's poetry translated by Nicholas Bethell (Longmans, 1967), and decided to try and meet Brodsky in Leningrad, his home city.

This was not difficult, as Leningrad's youth appeared to be one vast dissident cultural network who all knew each other, partied together, and ran a prolific *samizdat*. A foreigner in Moscow gave me the telephone number of someone in this network and before long people were ringing round to find out where Brodsky was and engineering a meeting with him. These young people had their own language for talking on the (tapped) telephone lines. Brodsky was referred to as 'n.v.r.' ('*nash velikii russkii*' – 'our great Russian'), or 'anglosex' (they claimed he was very fond of English girls).

Soon after arriving in Leningrad at the end of December, then, I was told to rendezvous with a young woman in a maxi-skirt somewhere in the city, and she took me by bus to a private house (I never discovered whose) where Brodsky was at that very moment.

We were ushered into a kind of conservatory at the back of the house, where the twenty-nine-year-old poet was sitting talking to three or four people. One was a quiet American male to whom he seemed close. Brodsky's face was striking: 'Very open, clean, tight face. Thinning hair. Gingerish sideboards and generally sandy complexion' (all quotations here are from an entry in my notebook at the time). Seamus Heaney's description of it, 'tawny containment', cannot be bettered.

Although Brodsky was smoking, and presumably relaxing, there was a tautness to him that verged on nervous agitation. He had just returned from Moscow. Someone asked if he had seen 'the widow' (Nadezhda Mandelstam). He had. He said that she was well and they had had a long talk, but he would not elaborate. Whether parts of Nadezhda Mandelstam's memoirs were then circulating in *samizdat*, I do not know; but everyone present understood that she could not be named or discussed, as there might be microphones even here. Palpable awe hung in the air, that he was so close to 'the widow'. A Russian subsequently confided that Nadezhda Mandelstam and Anna Akhmatova saw Brodsky as the inheritor of Osip Mandelstam's mantle as a Russian poet.

When my turn came to be introduced and talk to Brodsky, I committed one gaffe after another. He asked me what my literary research was on. When I replied 'Chekhov', he glazed over. Years later he explained that his schooling had portrayed Chekhov as a Soviet writer and that had repelled him, but in the West he had come to see Chekhov as one of the 'heights' of Russian culture. Next, when asked about modern Russian poetry, I said that I loved Pasternak's Peredelkino and Zhivago poems (I had not read any Mandelstam by then). This fell utterly flat. Brodsky would not say *anything* about Pasternak – presumably because Nadezhda Mandelstam's circle disapproved of Pasternak's 1934 'conversation with Stalin'. I offered Brodsky one of the best Soviet cigarettes, but he asked me how I could possibly smoke them and produced a packet of American ones. Finally, I asked him if I could consult him about two lines in Mayakovsky's 'Unfinished', which I was translating. Brodsky laughed and said that he was hardly the best person to consult about Mayakovsky. I had foreseen this, but wanted his opinion as I was sure only another poet could get at the lines' meaning. He then focused completely on the poem, told me how he interpreted the lines, and turning to the American said he was surprised at the quality of the piece.

I decided to ask Brodsky what he thought of Bethell's translations of him. 'He is a tough sheet,' he replied. I literally did not understand what he meant at first, because outside American English I think 'shit' was still used only of things. It was clearly one of Brodsky's favourite expressions, because when I asked him next what he thought of Voznesensky's verse, I was told he too was a 'sheet'. Yevtushenko, by contrast, was a 'sincere bloke', even though his verse was full of 'banalities'. The significant thing about this part of the encounter, I now think, is that my questions were about the poetry but the answers came about the men.

Above: Joseph Brodsky, 1969 (photographer unknown).
Right: 'Visit to Russia', 1969, autograph.

Altogether, I did not think the conversation was going anywhere. But at the end, Brodsky invited me to come and see him 'at home'. He gave me his address (Liteinyi 24, Flat 28) and told me to ring him during the week.

On 11 January 1970 I went by arrangement to a café off Nevsky. 'Iosif', as everyone called him, was there, talking to a few people and already standing ready to go. We made a party of four or five and Iosif set the pace as we hurtled along the streets, he in a well-worn western fur coat. As far as I could see, we were not being followed.

When we entered his room, which was dark and jam-packed with objects (I particularly remember a fencing mask), he motioned me to a long cloth-draped sofa. However, it was covered with airmail envelopes, letters and telegrams, and I wasn't sure whether I should clear them to sit down. He laughed. The litter, he explained, was 'congratulations on the New Year' and came from all over the world. One airmail was from Greece. 'You know, I have friends there. Have often visited the place. – Joking, of course!'. This painfully ironic statement was accompanied by a laugh that 'ended with him looking as though going to cry like a child'. He explained that his love of Greece was associated with Cavafy, whose poetry he greatly admired and recommended to me.

Another airmail on the sofa was from W.H. Auden and Brodsky told me to read it. As I recall, it was very friendly and even flattering. But Iosif was clearly wary. According to him, 'Auden's link-up with Voznesensky etc., his interest in young Russia[,] was generally explicable by his guilty hankering for his 1930s views'. Auden's leftism was 'a dormant illness'.

This led easily into Brodsky's judgement of the other greats of twentieth-century English poetry. Despite the fact that he had written a poem on the death of T.S. Eliot (inspired, it seems, by Auden's 'In Memory of W.B. Yeats'), he did not like Eliot's late verse. 'He killed the poet in himself.' Pound was completely alien: 'I don't like him/ understand what he is getting at.'

Reverting to the Auden theme, Brodsky asked me why I thought the West was so taken by the young Russian poets, what people over there saw in them, since they could only read them in translation. As it happened, I had recently been asking myself this question. In Leningrad I had even written a short poem in English 'To the Russian Poets'. So I simply asked Iosif for a sheet of paper, wrote the poem out, and gave it to him. He read it slowly, pursed his lips, and nodded. The poem suggested that the tradition of Russian poets as victims 'closed' them in 'aim and audience' and wasn't good for them; Iosif took the pen and wrote underneath that Western poets 'play in our pen / with loaded guns'.

He handed me the sheet and I was amazed to see his own poem was written in English. I found the way that he had taken the humorous limerick form and translated it into a serious Russian epigram extremely original, if challenging. We realised, however, that the themes of our two scraps of verse converged. After this exchange, he was much more relaxed with me.

By now other people were arriving. The afternoon was clearly developing into a salon. Brodsky made coffee for us, or poured out small glasses of Estonian liqueur. No one mentioned politics. I think this must have been because everyone had the same view of the regime and anyone who raised the subject would have been a provocateur. The expectation grew that Iosif would recite some poems. I jokingly suggested his 'Long Elegy to John Donne', which was his best-known poem in Britain but over two hundred lines long. He laughed this off and said he would recite his translation of Donne's 'The Apparition'.

It was magnificent. To my ear, Brodsky had a beautiful, searing voice and spoke with unobtrusive precision. It was both a literal translation and a masterly paraphrase. I was thrown by his rendering Donne's 'poor, Aspen wretch' as 'o my poor asp [viper]', because I was sure 'Aspen' referred to the tree and imaged trembling, but it would have been churlish to say so. The translation gave me the opportunity to ask Iosif why he was so attracted to Donne, who at the time was the English poet I read most. I assumed Donne had influenced the metaphysical nature of his verse and his highly un-Soviet use of enjambement. Reading Brodsky in Russian, I gained the impression he was 'drawing his pains / Through rhyme's vexation' ('The Triple Fool'). I was stunned, therefore, when he gave me a short, succinct answer. He translated

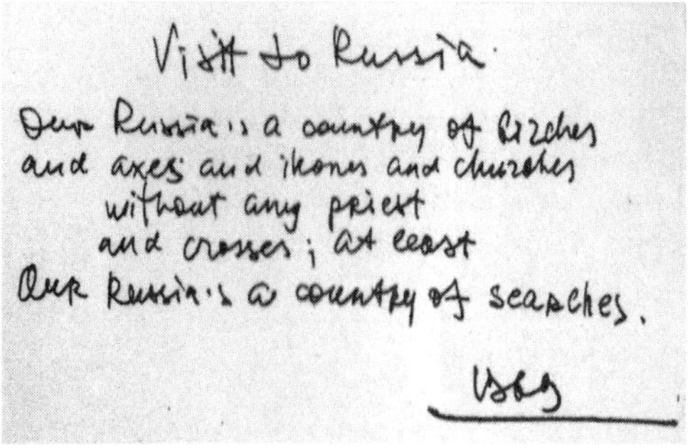

Donne because the latter 'represents a vital period in the development of Western Christianity since the Greeks'.

The 'salon' was plainly going to continue into the night, so having been the first to arrive I left after about three hours, but not before Iosif had given me a written recommendation to read the poetry of Hyam Plutzik: 'Everything which [was] published after 1956; especially that book which includes a poem called "Horatio".' I had never heard of the American poet Plutzik.

A month or two later, some girls from French universities whom I knew at a Moscow University student hostel visited Leningrad with the express purpose of meeting Brodsky, and I was very interested to hear their accounts. One intimated that she was having an affair with him. She said she asked Iosif why his poems were 'so long' (presumably the Donne elegy, 'Gorbunov and Gorchakov' etc). His reported reply could be translated literally as 'the longer it lasts, the better, I think, no?', but the Russian he used caused hilarity as it could also refer to lovemaking and she seemed unaware of that. The girls were fashionably left wing and he had apparently told them that all their thinking was 'received ideas' – which was true. He shocked them to the core by declaring that he wished the US would win the Vietnam War and carry on to Moscow.

In May 1970 I visited Leningrad again, but saw Brodsky only once, at a huge party containing the 'flower' of the city's intelligentsia. However, I was lent a sheaf of his poems in *samizdat* and some of them, especially 'Winter Evening in Yalta' and 'A Halt in the Desert', had a very powerful effect on me. I was followed everywhere. The next time I met Iosif was in London after his expulsion from the Soviet Union on 4 June 1972.

*

When I look back on that experience of Russian poetry *in situ*, so to speak, two issues strike me, which are sides of the same coin. No one would discuss the poetical or linguistic qualities of these poets; what made them individual, new, original, accomplished, or not; what made specific poems good, or not. None of their admirers seemed interested in doing this, or to have the language with which to do it. No one attempted to do it with Brodsky's oeuvre. People seemed carried away by the afflatus of their own perception of these poets as declaimers of truths, 'prophets', the latest incarnation of the Russian poet-martyr. I feel that in Leningrad the intelligentsia engaged not so much with Iosif's writing as with his personification of their own image of a 'great Russian poet'. It was this totemistic euphoria that bore him along – that gave him his celebrity. I wrote in my notebook a bit later: 'The image of the Russian poet overtook Brodsky too soon.'

But I am convinced that he himself was totally impervious to it, both then and later. At one of his last public readings (in New York), a Russian fan asked him: 'You are a Russian poet... Don't you want to return to your motherland, to replicate the destiny of Solzhenitsyn or Tsvetaeva?' Iosif replied: 'I certainly don't want to replicate Tsvetaeva's fate. And I have no desire to follow Solzhenitsyn's example, either. My life is my life, not the destiny of the Russian literary tradition.' He was absolutely right.

Emigration

PATRICK MILES
in memoriam Joseph Brodsky

'But how do I choose? How can I choose
from so many dresses? And I think:
perhaps I don't need a dress after all!'

She touched her henna, straightened, drew her legs
beneath her, paused, and folded down her hem.
The rush chair soughed. I saw an English gent
who broached some subject with a soft 'ahem'.

'Russian trains are so beautiful don't you think?
So big and spacious, made of wood and brass –
not like the claustrophobics you have here!
We took the train to Leningrad at night,
we had a jazz band, and all our wedding night
we danced the boogie-woogie!'

(Always with a squeeze of tears or laughter.)

'David will be home at eight.
Do you know how exciting, how spontaneous it is
to talk with body, and hands, and eyes,
when you have no words?
Perhaps we even knew each other better then,
without each other's language?'

She snatched a small Peruvian cushion:

'We had freedom in Russia!
You see, we didn't have to decide anything!'
(Pulling the cushion in her stomach.)

Here you *have* to do things, you have to pay your taxes,
you have to think!... Ah but here come my angels,
let me show you my angels,
come in, my angels!'
(Arms outstretched.)

A door swung back. They stood, toe-tip to threshold,
in white night-dresses. Flaxen. Purest Angles.
She glanced aside, as if to check a star
still hung among the dandruff east of Chelsea;
as you once put it, 'mathematically' far.

From the Archive

Issue 147, September–October 2002

R.F. LANGLEY

From the poem 'After the Funeral'.
Fellow contributors to this issue
include Carola Luther, Sinéad
Morrisey, Marilyn Hacker, Jeremy
Over, Geoffrey Hill and John Ashbery.

from AFTER THE FUNERAL

In the Ceramic Gallery. No train
till half past five. Yellow.

No amber. A hornet
would be something from another poem,
eager for nectar. We

fleer with yellow leaves. A
row of white bowls that make
mouths at it, months of it,
moon after moon. Colder
and rimmed with copper. In

the Ceramic Gallery, the yellow
October plane tree leaves in Gordon Square.
Nothing slabbered about Pauline's death. Some
details will rustle about or hump it
and call it a sixpenny jug. Think it
as leaves. Think it as bowls. It's a question [...]

Deposition

DAN BURT

Tumour

Surgeons probed the ruin
that six weeks ago was a woman
for the source of her Nile of pain:
razed ovaries through a keyhole –
they proved benign;
twice hoovered her guts
through a nasogastric hose –
but still they fouled;
slit the abdomen at last
and from her colon cut
the egg-sized ruby mass
that damned her bowels.

Post-Op

In the room scrubs come and go,
check vital signs, the glucose drip,
bring clear liquids for her to sip,
but tell us nothing we want to know.

Either side of the bed we stand,
spin bad news into bland,
walk off at times to hide
trembling lip, dampening eye,
and dread the 'path' report
will ferry hope to Hell.

Mid-morning, mid-afternoon,
the scarecrow hanging on my arm
shuffles speechless round the ward
while I hum *Va pensiero* under my breath,
conjure the orchestra, hear
Nabucco's Hebrew slaves implore
a God I'm certain is not there,
for strength to endure.

Delphi

Nine storeys up the January sun
fills the oncology waiting rooms,
lights pear wood chairs,
beige carpets, off-white walls,
and pencil-thin, pale alopetes,
whose cadaverous flesh
mocks the studied calmness.
Patient, daughter, and I sit,
fidget, prattle, go for a pee,
and feign no fear
the news will be
not what we want to hear.

The haruspex enters quietly,
half-tied surgical gown askew,
scuffed, brown wing-tipped shoes,
a shambling, portly, distant man
whose blank face, guarded gaze,
say he's acted the raven in too many plays:

You have Stage IV colon cancer. We couldn't find the source.
The surgeon who removed the blockage thinks he got it all,
but can't be sure. When you recover a little more, we'll do an
endoscopy, and PET scan; but I doubt they'll change our view.
Chemotherapy's standard for what you have, a six-month
course, if you can stand it. Then we review.

What will the chemo do?

Give you a year, maybe two....

Her late-life only child turns aside to sob;
I flinch, though the verdict's no surprise;
and my wasted, high school heart-throb,
poleaxed, mute, empty eyed,
decouples from us and, like a stranger,
boards her little black train.

Totentanz

Death settles on the exam table
as the oncologist bids good-day,
flutters anthracite feathers,
eyes us, then with a nod
swings his new partner away.

Wrapped in his grim wingspan
gyring down the shadow path,
she pries at the talons
that clamp her fast,
with chemicals, diet, all she can muster
to loosen them for a measure,
though nothing can ever dissever
this pair from their round together.

I am a wallflower at the dance
watching a lady slowly die,
and as sigh treads on sigh
replay a sixty-year-old teen romance.

Coda

She paused, looking at him for a moment with a
smile. 'My name? I am Mademoiselle Yvonne de Galais...'
Then she was gone.
Alain Fournier, 'Le Grand Meaulnes'

We trudged under the lash of measurement,
each pulse a question,
Will the next scan be clear?
pursued by odds we'd too soon hear
Your cancer is past treatment.

Against that hour I sifted memory
for the clarity a tango with extinction brings:
not the last ten winter years
when we grew close,
chance-met again after half a century,
but three months as your subject
while you slummed it,
a pubescent uptown rose
dallying with a bit of rough.

I refined myself
after that brief encounter,
quarried Wordsworth, Eliot, Lowell, Yeats,
cast your deities as mine,
pictured us kneeling at their shrine,
but the conjunctive moment past
worshipped alone.

I'll sing no sad songs for you,
my dearest, now you are dead,
instead for *kaddish* will surrender
the rage loving you engendered
and the still-born dreams that drove me
lee-rail buried down the years.

Jill Rubinson
(i.m. 17/8/1943 — 30/7/2018)

'My tennis improves'

DAVID HERMAN

Adam Kirsch, *Why Trilling Matters* (Yale University Press), 2011, 185pp, $24.00;
Adam Kirsch (ed.), *Life in Culture: Selected Letters of Lionel Trilling* (NY: FSG), 2018, 449pp, £35.00 hb

---

'ONLY YESTERDAY,' wrote Lionel Trilling in a letter in 1967, 'having asked a class of mine to read T.S. Eliot's *The Sacred Wood*, I found that they really couldn't understand anything of the situation out of which Eliot was writing. It was a shock to me, for the book had been of the greatest importance to me when I was in college. But after all, it had first appeared in 1920, forty-seven years ago, nearly half a century, which is a long time in literary culture.' Trilling was right. Half a century is a long time in literary culture. It is now about fifty years since he wrote this letter. What do we make of Trilling's reputation today?

For thirty years after the Second World War Trilling was the most influential literary critic in America. No American critic today enjoys the prestige Trilling enjoyed during those years. No wonder that it mattered so much to Edward W. Said that he should have Trilling's old office at Columbia. He knew what that office symbolised, at Columbia, but also far beyond.

And yet when I arrived at Columbia as a graduate

student in 1979 Trilling's reputation was already in decline, just four years after his death. Literary theory was at its heyday. Harold Bloom had just written *The Anxiety of Influence* (1973), Derrida's *Of Grammatology* had just been translated and Said had published *Beginnings* (1975) and *Orientalism* (1978). While I was in New York I attended talks by Borges, Foucault, Tzvetan Todorov and Susan Sontag. This was a different world from Trilling's genteel and Anglophone criticism. Adam Kirsch writes in *Why Trilling Matters*, 'when I was an undergraduate English major in the mid-1990s, I don't believe Trilling was ever assigned or discussed in any of my courses'.

Trilling's whole language of 'large and general words', in Kirsch's phrase, seemed out of date. All that talk of morality and liberalism. Take this passage on E.M. Forster: 'All novelists deal with morality, but not all novelists... are concerned with moral realism, which is not the awareness of morality itself but of the contradictions, paradoxes and dangers of living the moral life.' This seemed quaint and old fashioned to a young generation of students and academics. What did words like 'strenuous' and 'exigent' mean when it came to reading texts? A few years after he had died this whole language seemed like something from a museum of literary criticism. Eliot's *Sacred Wood* seemed alive and relevant by comparison.

It wasn't just about Trilling, of course. During the 1980s and '90s, that whole post-war generation of Jewish-American critics had not fared well either. Who read Irving Howe, Alfred Kazin or Leslie Fiedler? The moment of *Dissent* and *Partisan Review* had passed. They had become the subject of jokes in Woody Allen movies and had been replaced by new kids on the block like *Semiotexte*, *Yale French Studies* and *Critical Inquiry*.

But then came the Trilling revival. In 2000 *The Atlantic* published a piece by Nathan Glick on Trilling, 'The Last Great Critic', and Leon Wieseltier edited a collection of Trilling's essays, *The Moral Obligation to Be Intelligent*. In 2002 Adam Phillips wrote a brilliant essay on Trilling and his fascinating relationship with Arnold, James and Forster. Trilling's novel, *The Middle of the Journey*, and his best-known book of essays, *The Liberal Imagination*, were both republished in new editions in 2008. There were long profiles of Trilling and his wife Diana in *The New Yorker* and a biography of Diana appeared in 2017. In 2011 *Why Trilling Matters* was published, a passionate defence by Adam Kirsch, one of America's leading young critics. And now comes Trilling's *Selected Letters*, also edited by Kirsch. Is this revival of interest in Trilling, long overdue, a valuable reassessment of a great critic? *Does* Trilling matter? Or has Trilling's moment truly passed?

Lionel Mordecai Trilling was born in Queens in New York in 1905, the son of Fannie (née Cohen) and David Trilling, from Bialystok in Poland. His family was Jewish, part of that great tide of immigrants that came from east Europe and the Russian Pale to America between the early 1880s and the legislation restricting immigration in the early 1920s. His contemporaries included Leslie Fiedler, Alfred Kazin and Henry Roth, Malamud, Bellow and Arthur Miller.

But Trilling was not straightforwardly one of the 'first generation' Jewish intellectuals who came from immigrant families. In 1972 he wrote a fascinating letter about his family, in particular his mother. She was born and schooled in England and came to America in her teens. Her family, he wrote, 'were fairly comfortable'. 'Her mode of speech was very pure, without any trace of a foreign accent.' He went on, in the same letter, 'It was characteristic of my mother that all her life and especially in her late years she had close friends who were not Jewish.' 'Both parents', he wrote in the same letter:

> were devoted not merely to the idea of education as a means of advancement... but also to the idea of 'culture'. Of a life shaped by several kinds of amenity. My first books were from the family bookcase. I still have my mother's set of George Eliot, her favorite writer;... there were sets of Dickens, Thackeray, and Kipling and the Temple Shakespeare. My copy of *Sartor Resartus* was my father's.

He didn't go to City College, where so many of the New York Intellectuals were educated. Instead he went to Columbia. 'City College,' he wrote, 'was out of the question, for my parents as socially inferior...' He spent nearly all his career at Columbia, as an undergraduate, postgraduate and teacher for nearly forty years. The choice of Columbia over City College was to haunt his relationships with many of his contemporaries for decades. It contributed to the image of Trilling as a snob, a non-Jewish Jew, not one of us.

Trilling's un-Jewish name was, he wrote, 'a significant part of my life'. His mother's father was Israel Cohen. What would have become of Trilling if he had grown up in early twentieth century America with such a Jewish name? The Ivy League universities were riddled with anti-Semitism. In 1903, just before Trilling was born, Ludwig Lewisohn left Columbia without a PhD because of being a Jew. Two decades later, he noted that 'Prejudice has not... relented in a single instance in regard to the teaching of English'. As Edward Alexander observes in his review of Trilling's Letters in *Standpoint*:

> Perhaps this was because the study of English, unlike that of science or philosophy, was intimately bound up with the particularities of culture, for it was precisely the study of the mind of Western Christianity. What Bernard Berenson called the 'Angry Saxons' who ran English departments were determined to protect Tennyson's 'treasure of the wisdom of the West' from barbarous Eastern (European) invaders.

It was around the time when Lewisohn was looking back darkly on his own experience of anti-Semitism at Columbia, that Trilling arrived on Morningside Heights. 'In 1921, when I entered Columbia,' Trilling wrote towards the end of his life, 'the College was pretty far along toward its Jewish coloration... A quite large proportion of the student body was Jewish, but 'power' was still in the hands of non-Jews – clubs, publications, sports. Etc. None of our teachers was Jewish...'

In a much earlier letter, in 1929, Trilling wrote:

> I was pretty divorced from Jewish life or thought of any sort. I cannot remember that I made any extravagant flutterings or uttered cries of despair at being [word missing]. I was comfortable enough. On the one hand, I never received any personal

manifestations of anti-Semitism, and on the other, I found that I simply preferred my Jewish to my Gentile friends. I was not rebelling. I was merely ignoring. Implicit in my feeling about Judaism was that it was not unpoetic, but quite empty of meaning now and inclined to manifest itself stupidly.

This paragraph is a minefield. What strange phrases, 'extravagant flutterings', and 'cries of despair' that he 'cannot remember' uttering. 'I *simply* [my emphasis] preferred' Jewish friends to gentiles? Thirty years later Trilling co-edited Ernest Jones's famous biography of Freud down to a single volume and he wrote widely about Freud, especially in relation to literature. What would Trilling, later immersed in Freud, have made of these words? And then there is the final sentence. Judaism 'was not unpoetic, but quite empty of meaning now and inclined to manifest itself stupidly'. Why such hostility?

This letter is just the first of many by Trilling full of ambivalence and ambiguity about Jewishness and Judaism. As Robert Alter writes, Trilling 'never escaped his inner demons, and a good many of them seem to have been Jewish'.

Why, for example, were none of the characters in Trilling's novel, *The Middle of the Journey*, Jewish? As Adam Kirsch points out in *Why Trilling Matters*, the originals of figures like the Crooms and John Laskell were mostly Jews. Yet, as the very Jewish Leslie Fiedler pointed out, 'not one of the essential characters is, incredibly, a Jew, though much of the flavor of the Communist experience in America is their flavor'.

'I myself am chiefly interested in the fictional representation of the Jew,' Trilling writes in that same letter in 1929. It may have suited him to write this in a letter to the editor of *The Menorah Journal*, but was it true? Only in a very strange way. Kirsch quotes this passage from a piece by Trilling in that publication: 'As soon as the Jewish writer gets his hero to be a Jew, he wraps him up warm in a *talith* and puts him away... the Jewish hero is lifted out of life and made to goggle his eyes in functionless ecstasy at the fact that he is a Jew.'

But it is one thing to write about Jews (even in such a stereotyped way) in *The Menorah Journal*, but when he started writing for the mainstream it was a different story. His first books were about Matthew Arnold (1939) and E.M. Forster (1943), who could hardly have been more non-Jewish as subjects, despite Arnold's serious reflections on Hebraism and the Jews. And look at who Trilling wrote about in his breakthrough book of essays, *The Liberal Imagination* (1950): Sherwood Anderson, Henry James and *Huckleberry Finn*, Kipling, Wordsworth and Scott Fitzgerald. The only Jew he wrote about in the whole book was Freud. Of course, as a new generation of critics have pointed out since the 1980s, you don't have to be Jewish to write about 'the fictional representation of the Jew'. Writers like Scott, Dickens, George Eliot and Trollope were fascinated by Jews. But the point is that Trilling wasn't. Not in his fiction or in his criticism, except for a handful of essays, for example, on Isaac Babel and 'Wordsworth and the Rabbis'.

Of course, we should consider the context. When Trilling was writing about Arnold and Forster, he was a young academic in his thirties, starting out, a Jew in a gentile, even anti-Semitic, academic world. His parents suffered during the Depression and relied on their son financially through the 1930s. In an angry letter to his sister, Harriet, Trilling wrote in 1939, the year his book on Arnold was published:

It is now eight years, more or less, that I have been carrying the chief support of Mother and Father... In that time I have made that responsibility my chief concern... Indeed, I think that since I first undertook it I have not been wholly out of debt; nor am I now.

In 1936 Trilling was temporarily dismissed from the English Department at Columbia. He was a Jew, a Marxist, a Freudian. His PhD supervisor, Emery Neff, reportedly complained that Trilling had 'involved himself with ideas', that he was 'overly sensitive' and didn't really 'fit [in] because he was a Jew'. It is perhaps not surprising that Trilling played safe with two such respectable subjects as Matthew Arnold and E.M. Forster.

And by the 1940s when he was writing the essays collected in *The Liberal Imagination*, it was the height of the Cold War. Trilling was not just a Jew, he had flirted with Communism in the 1930s. He had only just been promoted to full professor at Columbia. It was not a time to rock the boat with books or even essays on the representation of Jews in literature.

But what about *Sincerity and Authenticity* (1972), based on the Charles Eliot Norton Lectures he gave at Harvard in 1969–70? By then Trilling was at the height of his career, the most acclaimed literary critic in America. Marx and Freud loom large, but they are the only Jewish figures who do. There are a few passing references to Walter Benjamin (mentioned twice), Bellow and Roth (once each).

Trilling's lack of interest in Jews as a subject did not go unnoticed in the very Jewish world of the New York Intellectuals. In a 1961 letter to the art critic, Clement Greenberg, Trilling recalls a bitter argument ('our heated encounter') between the two men back in 1945 when Greenberg had accused him of Jewish self-hatred. 'I certainly was as angry at you as I have ever been at anyone,' Trilling writes. The following month, Trilling writes to Greenberg again: 'I feared and disliked everything I knew about American Jewish life, and maybe more than that.'

Trilling may not have been interested in Jews in literature. What about his own Jewishness? In 1944 he contributed to a symposium in the *Contemporary Jewish Record* on 'American Literature and the Younger Generation of American Jews'. In *Why Trilling Matters*, Kirsch quotes Trilling's words: 'I do not think of myself as a "Jewish writer". I do not have it in mind to serve by my writing any Jewish purpose. I should resent it if a critic of my work were to discover in it either faults or virtues which he called Jewish.'

The following year he writes in a letter, 'So many of my feelings [about Jewish life] are negative'. In 1947, he writes, 'But so far as I can make out – and I think I have a lively awareness of Jewish life – there are now in America no special Jewish values of a large and important sort, such as there have been at earlier times in Jewish history.' In the same letter, he writes, 'I know many Jews of large mind and morality, but I do not know of a single mind in Jewish life that speaks as a Jew and with any intellectual authority in the exposition of Jewish values.'

In a letter to Rabbi Max Kadushin in 1952, Trilling writes, 'Part of the difficulty is of course my lack of familiarity with your points of reference and the names for things.' As if to prove his point, he misspells Halakha as 'Halabah'. This misspelling happens elsewhere. In 1958 he misspells *shtetlach* as *stetloch* and *mikveh* as *mitzvah*. In the same letter, far more troubling are his comments on Jews and sexuality. '[T]hey think that sex is dirty, that all the body is dirty,' he writes. '[H]ow disturbed by sex the Jews are.' And Jewish culture revolts him:

> I don't share your enthusiastic admiration for Jewishness as it appears in East European Jewry. No, I don't – I find that each year I regard it with more and more adversity. [...] I grow less and less sympathetic with almost all of the manifestations of the culture. [...] Nor do I like the culture any better in its attenuated American forms. I think it has injured all of us dreadfully. Does this shock you?

Judaism fares no better. Rabbis 'don't engage me', he wrote to Kadushin in 1952. They aroused 'very little sympathy or fellow feeling'. 'Very little in Jewish religious life speaks to me.' Jewish theology 'engages me less than any other' (1965) and 'my alienation from Judaism is in large part an irritable response to the unsatisfactoriness – the dimness – of its theological utterances' (1965). This hostility towards Jews and Judaism recurs through his letters throughout the post-war period.

Then there is the absence of Nazism in his letters in the 1930s. There is a letter to Columbia about their invitation to the German ambassador to speak at the university (11 December 1933) and a single reference to Nazism during the war (21 September 1943), but that's it. There are almost no references to the Second World War itself and just one to the Holocaust. On 12 August 1941, just after the German invasion of the Soviet Union, Trilling writes to his friend and colleague, Jacques Barzun, 'There is no news except that my tennis improves'.

During the War Trilling is mostly concerned with his book about Matthew Arnold (1939) and recent articles ('I have just sent you a copy of my Wordsworth paper', 12 August 1941; 'If you get to see the current *Partisan Review*, do look at a piece of mine', 10 May 1942; 'The only interesting thing that has happened to me since we last met is that *Time* magazine offered me its literary editorship', 18 June 1942).

As the war comes to an end, he writes just once about the death camps: 'Together with the stories of the great demolitions have come the stories of the atrocity camps, and people are talking a great deal about them, very deeply disturbed, more disturbed, I think, than they are conscious of yet trying to bring their sense of the thing to consciousness...' (6 May 1945). 'And as for an attitude toward the atrocity-camp stories, that I find very nearly hopeless. When they began coming in, there were days when I wondered why I was so unutterably tired and unable to get anything done...' (ibid).

Nor is he much more interested in the Holocaust in later years. There is one extraordinary moment when he writes in 1960 of 'my long continuing desire to write a history of the last days of the Warsaw ghetto, really a history'. Since he didn't read German, Polish or Yiddish, and never mentions any historians of the Holocaust except for one reference to Hannah Arendt, it is not clear what kind of 'history' this would have been. Israel barely registers either (one single reference). There is no discussion of Zionism and almost none of Yiddish literature or culture.

Perhaps most surprising is Trilling's lack of interest in Jewish-American writing. There are exceptions. In 1953 he wrote that he had just finished the galleys of *The Adventures of Augie March*. 'I'm delighted with it and enormously impressed.'

But in the unedited transcript of Bellow's interviews with Philip Roth (2 December 1999), Bellow says that Trilling was 'dead against' *Augie March*:

> After Bellow showed Trilling the first hundred or so pages, Trilling's reaction was, 'It's very curious, it's very interesting but somehow it's wrong.' This reaction Bellow calls 'the academic view.' Roth then asks Bellow if he thinks Trilling was 'blind to the Americans?' by which he means the American language, the language of the American street. Bellow answers that Trilling 'didn't have much feeling for it'.

Nor, Roth adds, did Trilling have much understanding of Bellow's sense of himself as a Jew. According to Roth:

> there was a way of being a Jew and that was Trilling's way, but this [Bellow's way] was a strange way because it was both a way out and a way in. Because it wasn't just that you were finding a way out of being a Jew; you were finding a way as a writer into being a Jew without doing what Malamud did.

This is interesting. How could American writers find a way as a writer into being a Jew? This was a question which fascinated Bellow and Roth. It doesn't seem to have interested Trilling ever.

And when *Herzog* was due to be published in 1964, Trilling wrote to Bellow's publisher, Pascal Covici, that it wouldn't be possible for him to review it for *The New York Times* ('I am still at work finishing my bedamned anthology... and of course I mustn't allow anything to interfere with that'). But he then goes on to say, 'Not that it would have been an easy piece' because 'I experienced the foreboding of disappointment, which – I'm afraid I have to tell you – fulfilled itself'.

In his new biography of Bellow, Zachary Leader points out that Trilling supported a renewal of Bellow's Guggenheim Fellowship and praised Bellow on the eve of publication of *Augie March*. He also documents the tensions between the two men and the occasional contretemps that ensued.

Leader points out that the critic Alfred Kazin 'shared Bellow's distrust of Trilling'. In his memoir, *New York Jew*, '*the* barrier' between himself and Trilling is said to be the latter's fondness for the words 'scarcely', 'modulated', and 'our educated classes'. Bellow, according to Kazin, 'could never get over Trilling's "nerveless compromised accents", a tone that owed much to a reverence for Henry James'. This goes back to the Columbia vs City College choice. These working-class Jews, who grew up speaking Yiddish, saw Trilling as a snob, someone whose prose wore a three-piece suit.

Again, it's the absences that are more troubling. Trilling is writing during the heyday of the post-war Jewish-

American novel and yet there are barely any references to Mailer (six), Malamud (two), Arthur Miller (one). None to Heller, Roth or Grace Paley. There is one letter to Cynthia Ozick (about Forster's homosexuality not about her writing) and one to Susan Sontag, who had just sent him a copy of her new novel, *Death Kit* (1967). He thanks her for sending it. 'You will not be surprised, I fear, if I tell you that I am having trouble with it: you probably know how fixed in the past my taste in novels is.'

What emerges from the *Selected Letters* is that Trilling saw himself as a kind of Paleface (Arnold, Forster, James, lectures at Harvard) to these Jewish Redskins, all sons and daughters of east European and Russian immigrants. As he wrote, 'I rejected the way of chutzpah and mishegas in favour of reason and diffidence.'

There are other significant absences that run through *The Letters*. Trilling was curiously uninterested in European critics and intellectuals. Barely a handful of references to Benjamin, Lukács and Nietzsche. None to Adorno. Contemporary developments in criticism barely interest him. Theory doesn't feature at all. No Hartman, Bloom or Said, already major names by the end of Trilling's life. It's as if they didn't exist. Though he paid a number of visits to England, critics like Leavis, Empson and Steiner barely register and Kermode and Williams not at all. His *Letters* are like the famous cartoon of a New Yorker's view of America. Everything shrinks as you get further from Manhattan.

It's not just European critics. Except for Flaubert and Proust, he's not very interested in European writers either. No references to Isaac Babel (despite his famous essay on *Red Cavalry*) or Camus, Beckett or Orwell. Just a couple of references to Sartre and Kafka. 'I do not know Brecht,' he wrote in 1946. 'As for Sartre, I am too entirely ignorant of him to know how to judge [William] Barrett's estimate,' he wrote in the same year. He didn't make his first visit to Europe until 1956, when he was already in his fifties. For Trilling, it was English and American non-Jews writing between the early nineteenth century and the Second World War that counted: Wordsworth and Keats, Lawrence, Joyce and Yeats, T.S. Eliot and Dickens. When he is asked to nominate writers for the Nobel prize the three he chooses are all British or American: Robert Frost, E.M. Forster and Auden. Auden was almost sixty at the time, Frost and Forster were both in their mid-eighties.

But no women. There are the two letters to Sontag and Ozick, a few passing references to Lillian Hellman and Mary McCarthy and none to Elizabeth Hardwick, Sylvia Plath or Virginia Woolf. Even major male post-war writers slipped through the net. Almost nothing on Faulkner, Hemingway and Graham Greene, Auden, Pound or William Carlos Williams. Nothing at all on Berryman and Lowell, Nabokov, Tennessee Williams or Vidal.

What *is* at the centre of Trilling's world? His wife, Diana, above all, though not in a very illuminating or flattering way. There are no detailed readings of any of her essays or reviews. Columbia, *Partisan Review*, *Commentary* and *The Nation* matter to him. Forster and Arnold, of course, the subjects of his first two books, and Henry James, the three Paleface gentiles at the heart of Trilling's literary imagination. Freud too, though he's not very interested in other psychoanalysts, American or European.

Then there's Trilling the critic. Never mind who he reads, *how* does he read? 'In his major essays,' Kirsch concedes, 'he does not bring news of important new writers or teach us how to read difficult new works, the way Edmund Wilson does. Nor does he offer a polemical revaluation of literary history, the way F.R. Leavis does.' George Steiner changed the way literary academics thought about the Holocaust. Geoffrey Hartman, Gabriel Josipovici and Robert Alter transformed the way we think about the Hebrew Bible. A younger generation of Jewish, women and postcolonial critics changed the literary canon for good. Trilling, by contrast, didn't change the canon and didn't change the way we read. Yes, he championed Arnold and Forster, and Adam Phillips is extremely good on this in his brilliant essay, 'A Concentrated Rush'. How they helped Trilling find his voice. What they allowed him to say and freed him from not facing. But in the last years of his life, Trilling looked so old-fashioned compared to many of his contemporaries, never mind the new and rising generation. Trilling was almost totally ignorant of popular culture. 'What is *Batman?*' he wrote to his student Allen Ginsberg in 1945. Film didn't interest him and certainly television didn't.

More important for a literary critic, he was not a close reader. In his Introduction to *The Letters*, Kirsch quotes Irving Howe on Trilling and the New York Intellectuals:

> The kind of essay they wrote was likely to be wide-ranging in reference, melding notions about literature and politics, sometimes announcing itself as a study of a writer or literary group but usually taut with a pressure to go beyond its subject, toward some encompassing moral or social observation.

As Trilling himself said, 'My own interests lead me to see literary situations as cultural situations, and cultural situations as great elaborate fights about moral issues, and moral issues as having something to do with gratuitously chosen images of personal being.' Or as he wrote about *The Liberal Imagination*, 'these essays although essays chiefly in literature, all point beyond literature, to what we call life itself'.

This partly explains his huge popularity. *The Liberal Imagination* is said to have sold more than seventy thousand copies in hardcover and more than a hundred thousand in paperback. As Louis Menand writes, 'It did something that very few books have ever done: it made literary criticism matter to people who were not literary critics.' And it did this largely because it was not about close readings of difficult texts. It was about politics, culture and morality and popular mainstream authors.

There are other explanations that Kirsch doesn't address in *Why Trilling Matters* or in his Introduction to the *Selected Letters*. First, the writing is so accessible. Trilling, like Leavis, Edmund Wilson and Steiner, was a world away from today's literary academics with their ferocious jargon. This was criticism that ordinary audiences could read. More a higher kind of journalism.

Second, Trilling was writing at the heyday of literary criticism. '*The Liberal Imagination*,' wrote Menand in *The New Yorker*, 'belongs to the age of (it feels a little funny just typing the words today) heroic criticism. It sent literature into battle.' But he was also writing from a very privileged position. He wasn't hidden away in the sticks at some unknown university. He was writing in New York, at a famous Ivy League University, mainly for publications based in New York. He was quick to pick up on the popularity of Freud and psychoanalysis. He didn't write about obscure authors or ideas. He was political but not *too* political, certainly not too left wing, and fell out of favour in the sixties, during the student unrest. He was Jewish but not *too* Jewish. He was erudite without rocking the boat, either in the way he wrote or in his choice of subject matter. 'I am very largely an oldfashioned humanist', he wrote in a letter in 1945.

In 1957 Trilling wrote to Edmund Wilson, 'Two *general* critics. Two *American* critics. Two critics not *New* – yet, of course, not *old*.' 'Two *American* critics.' This was important too. Trilling was writing at the highpoint of the American Century, a term coined at the time he was writing some of the essays that appeared in *The Liberal Imagination*. After the war, America needed to be culturally great as well as politically great and so you get Abstract Expressionism, great new American writers, playwrights and composers and even great new American critics. And Trilling was the great new American critic at exactly the same time as Pollock was the great American painter, Aaron Copland and Leonard Bernstein were the great American composers and Bellow and Miller were the great American writers. Trilling never had the impact in Britain or Europe that he had in America. Today's revival is very much an American phenomenon. It barely exists outside the east coast.

And there's the Cold War. *The Liberal Imagination* was a Cold War book. Trilling was by then an anti-Communist. 'I live with a deep fear of Stalinism at my heart,' he wrote to the theatre critic, Eric Bentley, in 1946. 'I think of my intellectual life as a struggle, not energetic enough, against all the blindnesses and malign obfuscations of the Stalinoid mind of our time.'

It was a Cold War book in a second sense. It was as American as Copland or Miller. The first essay is called 'Reality in America'. Then comes Sherwood Anderson. Later there are essays on James, *Huckleberry Finn* and F. Scott Fitzgerald. It was the right book at the right time and it made Trilling the most famous critic in America.

The qualities that made Trilling so popular in the 1940s and '50s are precisely the qualities that led to attacks on him in the '60s and then his disappearance in the theory years. Kirsch argues that Trilling matters. Not anymore. Partly because the circumstances that came together and made him matter during the Cold War have changed. The heyday of literary criticism has gone. Literary criticism doesn't matter to the general reader as it once did. That Anglophone parochialism doesn't read so well today. Jewish critics and readers don't want Jewish intellectuals who didn't care about Israel or the Holocaust, Judaism or Yiddish, Miller, Bellow or Roth. Women readers and critics don't want to read literary critics who don't care about women writers and gay readers might raise an eyebrow about a critic who wrote a book about E.M. Forster but didn't realise he was gay till thirty years later. Trilling's *Selected Letters* will not win him many fans. Too much of what's there is disturbing and too much of what isn't there is even more disturbing.

Procuring Poetry

CHARLES BERNSTEIN

after Carlos Drummond de Andrade (1945)
& after John Yau and Michael Palmer

No fake verses about what's going on.
No creation or death before poetry.
Compared to which, life's a static sun,
with no heat or illumination.
Affinities, anniversaries, personal anecdotes – don't matter.
No fake poetry with the body,
an excellent, complete and comfortable body – senseless for poetry.

Your spleen, your fits of pleasure or pain in the dark – make no difference.
Don't share with me your feelings,
which reek of equivocation and beat around the bush.
What you think and feel, that is not yet poetry.

No singing about your city – leave it in peace.
Songs aren't machine music or family secrets;
and they're not music heard in passing
nor rumors of the sea on streets lined with spume.

Song's not nature
or community.
Storm and light, fatigue, fright – are of no importance for song.
Poetry – no taking poetry from things! –
elides subject and object.

No dramatising, no invocations,
no nagging. No wasted time lying.
No belaboring.
Your ivory yacht, your diamond slippers,
your manias and mazurkas, your family skeletons,
disappear in time's tunnels, worthless.

No reworking
your buried and melancholy childhood.
No oscillating between mirror and
disappearing memories.
What disappeared wasn't poetry.
What broke was no crystal.

Penetrate, with stealth, words' dominion.
Poems are waiting to be written.
They are paralysed but without despair.
Calm, fresh, membrane intact.
Mute and brute, immaculate as a dictionary.

Let the poem live within you, then write it.
Be patient with obscurity. Calm down when provoked.
Wait for each poem to become real, consummated
with the power of words
and the power of silence.

No forcing a poem out of limbo.
No picking a lost poem off the floor.
No adulating a poem. Accept it
like it accepts its concrete form concentrated
in space.

Each one
has a thousand secret faces under the surface
that ask you, without interest in the reply –
bad or worse – that you devise:
Did you bring the key?

Notice:
bereft of melody and conceit,
words, still humid, pregnant in sleep,
hide in the night, tumbling in a difficult river
transformed to scorn.

Three Poems

JODIE HOLLANDER

The Worry Book

In the worry book I write down all my worries,
so I don't have to worry all the time.
But I worry when I write down all my worries
that I might not be writing the right worries,
or I worry I may have forgotten a worry or two.
And I worry people will know how much I worry
and worry my worrying will make them worry.
You see how worrying worrying can be?
It makes me worry: will my worrying make me ill,
give me cancer: now that's pretty worrying.
But then I worry: these aren't rational thoughts;
and I worry about the hours I waste worrying,
which turns to months and years, more worrying,
which makes me think of death, the ultimate worry.
And then I start to worry about how I'll die.
I worry it might hurt, and worry I'll be worried
that no one will be there to hear my worries.
And what about after death: what if I'm still worried?
Will there be a book to write down all my worries,
so that I don't have to worry all the time?

Two Horses

Macedon Range, Australia

There is no happiness
like the happiness of horses.
Just look at these two beauties
moving through this landscape –
who has sent them to us,
and from what other world?
Today I'm watching them
meandering together
beside the Acacia trees.
As they pause to eat grass,
I see their long tails
swaying in the sunlight,
and I wonder what they know
of life that I don't know.
I've seen them stand for hours,
it doesn't really matter
whether the rains are coming,
or if that familiar darkness
will soon be on its way.
Seeing them here today
under this vast Australian sky
it finally dawns upon me:
my life is more than enough,
to be alive is a blessing.

And What If in the End He's Just a Bird?

A handsome bird at that, you know the type:
a bright pink crest, a coat of gorgeous orange,
perhaps you've seen the likes of him in shops,
and thought, *I'd like to bring this fellow home.*
And so one day you do, and well why not
spend your pennies on something beautiful?
So you buy the little guy, buy his brass cage too,
set up your brand new pet beside the window,
ensuring he'll look out to the sweeping views.
But right away the creature starts to shriek,
and shrieks all night, worse than an ailing child.
So you bring him food, bring him more fresh water,
shine his cage, even buy him toys and treats.
When nothing works, you take him to the vet,
who only smiles and says he's perfectly fine.
Later you wonder: perhaps he's feeling trapped
so you open up his cage, and say *fly free* –
But nope it's not that, he will not to budge;
so after deliberation you finally decide
the poor guy must be miserable here with me.
And yet he knows you plan to take him back,
and begins flying violently around his cage.
When you see him bleed, you rush over to help,
then he drives his claws directly into your neck –
Now you're bleeding too, and you're shrieking,
but funny how he's suddenly gone silent,
he's got you now exactly where he wants you:
no store will take an injured creature back;
and now you're wounded too, so you're a pair –
So you spend your hours tending just to him,
stroke him all day long, say he's handsome;
though in truth he's just a five-inch thing –
and already beginning to bag around the eyes.
Nevertheless, you're trapped with the little bastard
hopping around his cage, incessantly pecking
at the small rectangular mirror hanging inside.

Three Poems

Joe Carrick-Varty

Lop Nur

My father dives headfirst into a lake,
swims till his pink shoulders become stars.
He swims for days, beach to beach.

The pink shoulders of my father's stars
are attached to other stars by invisible rope.
Birds perch on them. Cranes and gulls

and bony blue herons appear at 6 a.m.
from behind the mountain, slipping
like moons, more the more you look.

My headfirst dive's no match.
Feel the gulp that's coming, barnacle-
chinned, the birds inexplicably lifting.

Moonless June

For weeks they arrive out of the Arctic Ocean,
watched by a grizzly momma and her cubs,
my father in a sky blue suit,
long sideburns, Elvis Costello glasses,
my giggling sister on his shoulders.
For weeks they cross the beach. For weeks
they reach the treeline, my sister
an old woman and my father a baby
swaddled in the suit. She rests for breath,
leans her one free arm against a boulder. The cubs
have stopped noticing; momma drinks
from a stream, paws at the moonless water.
My sister drops the suit, hears it land, breathes
like a woman I have never met.

When you lean close and tell me

not a day goes by that you don't think of him
but you're thinking less now and you hope this is a sign
I pick at the grass and remember all the people

I've thought about since this conversation started –
an ex from school, Sylvia upstairs, the postman.
When I exit the roundabout behind an ASDA lorry

it's not the A342 Northbound I'm driving on but the
freckled curve of my father's spine. When a stranger
spots them from the layby, points a gloved hand

to the horses drinking from the lake of my father's face
I climb the field to get a better view. In the valley
two leafless trees fill with light, become lungs.

Stripped Naked by the Flames

ANDY CROFT

'I now believe that there is an absolute incompatibility between art and private property.'
John Berger

I HAVE NEVER SEEN so many people at a poetry festival, so many television cameras – or so many Kalashnikovs. Two years ago I was in the southern Iraqi city of Basra with my friend the poet Amarjit Chandan. We were guests of the Iraqi Writers Union for the thirteenth annual Al-Marbed International Poetry Festival.

Dedicated to the late Iraqi poet and communist Mehdi Mohammad Ali, the festival attracted almost a hundred poets, amateurs and professionals, from Morocco, Tunisia, Egypt, Bahrain, Yemen, Iran, Kuwait, Sudan, Iraq, Assyria, Lebanon, Syria and the Iraqi diaspora scattered across the world.

During a week of readings and debates, poetry and music, we visited the birthplace of Basra's most famous poet Badr Shakir al-Sayyab, as well as the Basra international football stadium. There was a showing of the film *Samt al-Rai* (*The Silence of the Shepherd*) introduced by its director Raad Mushatat. One of the festival readings took place on the Shatt al-Arab waterway, on board a river-boat built for Saddam Hussein.

But the festival was taking place in a deadly context. Iraqi forces were still fighting Daesh/ISIS in the north. The billboards by the side of the roads advertised, not consumer-goods, but the faces of young men from Basra who had died fighting Daesh. Each night we were woken by the sound of gunfire marking the repatriation of local boys killed fighting in Mosul.

With a heavily armed security presence at all the readings, it was hardly surprising that the festival was a serious-minded affair. Most of the poets recited long poems, often from memory and usually about the suffering and grief of the Iraqi people. One man read a poem about the death of his son, killed fighting in Fallujah. Another compared Iraqi children to a forest of young trees cut down before they are full grown. One poet observed that every Iraqi child has an older brother called Death. Another described the poor of the world as the fuel that keeps the endless fires of war burning. There was a long poem about a local teacher who was badly injured by a Daesh car-bomb; although she managed to crawl out of the car, she realised that her clothes were on fire and that her modesty before God was threatened, so she climbed back into the burning car to die.

In the circumstances, the banner in the Basra International Hotel declaring that 'Poetry is the Present and Future of Basra' was a defiant assertion of the enduring importance of poetry in Iraqi society, its relationship to shared ideas of nation, faith, language and history. Arabic poetry has a 'yearning' music, descending cadencies and distinct metrical patterns, each intended for a different emotional delivery, and designed to invite audience participation. At some of the evening readings there were over a thousand people, men and women, young and old, frequently interrupting the poets with shouts and gestures of appreciation and applause. A six year old boy recited, entirely from memory, a ten minute-long poem comparing Iraq to a grieving woman.

The idea of a publicly-owned, serious and shared poetic tradition clearly persists across all classes in Arab culture. Television shows like *Million's Poet* and *Prince of Poets* regularly attract millions of viewers. Writers like Mahmoud Darwish, Adonis, Badr Shakir al-Sayyab and Ahmed Shawki are known and their poetry enjoyed by audiences a long way beyond the world of literature, and beyond the limits of literacy.

According to ALESCO (the Arab League Educational, Scientific and Cultural Organisation), twenty-seven percent of people in the Arab world cannot read or write. Six million Iraqis – twenty percent of the population – are illiterate. But poetry is older than literacy; its historical role is to say in memorable ways those things which society needs to hear and to remember. It is only in mass-literate societies that poetry becomes diminished in importance and seriousness.

In the UK – the world's first mass-literate society – writing has long been professionalised. The result is the commodification of poetry, the privatisation of feeling and the high educational entry requirements of our cultural institutions. Large parts of the contemporary British poetry 'industry' are embarrassingly trivial and self-important, characterised by snobbery, narcissism, humourlessness and political indifference.

Despite the ritual assertions of poetry's popularity – 'Brits have rekindled their love of verse,' 'the Cinderella of literary forms is back,' 'Poetry sales soar as political millennials search for clarity,' 'A new generation of female writers has attracted millions of online followers and an increasingly diverse audience,' 'With soaring sales and a younger, broader audience, poetry is on a high,' etc – sales of poetry books last year represented less than 0.7 percent of all book sales in the UK.

Every January the broadsheets announce the best books that are going to be published in the coming twelve months. Of course no-one has read all these books, since most of them have not yet been published (several do not even have titles). Nor, it is fair to assume, has anyone read all the tens of thousands of unpublished books that are *not* on these lists. The *Guardian*'s 'Best Books of 2017' included only eight poetry books – all but two of which were from Faber's catalogue. The paper's 'literary calendar' for 2018 managed to include just seven books of poetry (out of a recommended list of ninety-two titles); this year the *Guardian* could only find nine poetry books worth including on their list of the one hundred and fifty-two books 'you'll be reading this year'.

But the gate-keeping institutions intent on discovering the next poetry revival seem to be rather less interested in poetry than they are in poets. The most notable aspect

From the Archive

Issue 147, September–October 2002

MARILYN HACKER

From the poem 'Elegy for a Soldier: June Jordan, 1936–2002'. Fellow contributors to this issue include Carola Luther, Sinéad Morrisey, R.F. Langley, Jeremy Over, Geoffrey Hill and John Ashbery.

from ELEGY FOR A SOLDIER

The city where I knew you was swift.
A lover cabbed to Brooklyn
(broke, but so what) after the night shift
in a Second Avenue
diner. The lover was a Quaker,
a poet, an anti-war
activist. Was blonde, was twenty-four.
Wet snow fell on the access
road to the Manhattan Bridge. I was
neither lover, slept uptown.

[...]

of the row following Rebecca Watts' review of Hollie McNish's *Plum* in these pages is that both the *Guardian* and Radio Four saw it as a *news story about poets* rather than an arts story about poetry and literary criticism ('Poetry world split over polemic').

While corporate publishers compete to establish a hierarchy of poets based on their own lists, angry mobs squabble on social-media over the ownership of poetry. The result is a kind of privatisation-grab and a closing down of debate and enquiry. This has been exacerbated by the recent and somewhat unlikely involvement of Higher Education institutions (during one of the recent plagiarism rows a friend told me that was forbidden from expressing an opinion on any of the issues involved by the legal department of the university where he teaches).

National Poetry Day is less a celebration of poetry than of the PR machinery of corporate publishers. As Michael Schmidt has argued, 'poetry prizes are now the vehicle of literary reception. Control the prizes and you control the culture of reception'. The apparatus of celebrity book-festivals, 'controversial' short-lists and prize-giving ceremonies is designed to guarantee access to the financial rewards of poetry (commissions, contracts, festivals, university teaching posts, more prizes, etc).

The news drama around these prizes usually follows the same creaking narrative of major names, newcomers, bookies' favourites, outsiders and dark-horses. This has recently been enlivened by rows about identity ('TS Eliot prize row: is winner too young, beautiful – and Chinese?', 'Ode to whiteness: British poetry scene fails diversity test', 'Forward prize, backward reading: who grumbles if white writers win awards?', 'Why the T.S. Eliot prize shortlist hails a return to the status quo', 'Forward poetry prizes announce trailblazing shortlists,' etc).

But of course, *none of this has anything to do with poetry*. British cultural life has *always* been distorted by vested interests, social class, geography and political quietism, dominated by social groups wholly unrepresentative of British society and untypical of most people who read and write poetry. Until recently cultural privilege defended its investments behind words like 'tradition', 'standards' and 'taste'. In the absence of an agreed vocabulary for discussing poetry every prize-winning collection is now 'bold,' 'dark,' 'sassy,' 'daring,' 'honest,' 'audacious,' 'authentic,' 'personal' and 'brave'. These days power has to dress up in democratic rags in order to get what it wants and to keep what it already possesses.

When a few years ago the Poetry Book Society announced the 'Next Generation Poets' it was with the usual fanfare of self-congratulation and wild applause. The poets involved in the promotion are the 'most exciting new poets from the UK and Ireland'. Not only are they 'doing something new,' 'tackling fresh subject matter,' taking 'emotional and literary risks', and 'reinvigorating the poetry scene', these poets are 'expected to dominate the poetry landscape of the coming decade' and lead 'our national cultural conversation for many years to come.' People who make fatuous claims about 'dominating the poetry landscape' should remember Auden's reminder that it is the responsibility of poets 'to defend the language against corruption,' otherwise 'people lose faith in what they hear'.

British literary life would certainly be a little less dull if real cultural power (not just the composition of competition judging panels) were more widely diffused. Personally I would like to see more working-class poets in print, fewer critics who have been to university, more publishers based outside London, and fewer poets with Creative Writing MAs. But this is not, I think, what calls for greater diversity usually mean.

The *Guardian* recently brought us the exciting news that 'a passion for politics, particularly among teenagers and young millennials, is fuelling a dramatic growth in the popularity of poetry.' This followed on from the announcement in the paper a few months earlier that poetry is now 'the coolest thing' and that 'young rebel poets' from the 'emerging underground' are at last 'breaking the mould of traditional, more elitist verse'. Of the three 'young rebel poets' from the 'underground poetry scene' acclaimed by the *Guardian*, one was a beneficiary of the Poetry Society's Next Generation promotion and short-listed for the Costa Prize; one has been published by Penguin; the other is published by Simon and Schuster.

There are a great many poets writing today whose work might properly be described as rebellious or underground. But they are not very likely to be recognised by the gate-keepers at the *Guardian* or *Poetry Review*.

Smokestack Books was established in 2004 with the explicit intention of publishing oppositional, dissident, unfashionable and radical poets. Smokestack's declared aim is to keep open a space for what is left of the socialist and communist poetic traditions in the twenty-first century, publishing books that otherwise would be unlikely to appear in print, and putting into English poets whose work is either unavailable or unknown in the UK.

To date Smokestack has published one hundred and sixty titles and sold over forty-four thousand books, including John Berger's *Collected Poems*, Louis Aragon's last book, *Les Chambres*, Mayakovsky's epic *Lenin*, three collections for grown-ups by Michael Rosen, a translation by Tom Leonard of Brecht's *Mother Courage*, the collected lyrics of Victor Jara, two book-length poems by Yiannis Ritsos, poets from Venezuela, Poland, the Netherlands, Italy, Bulgaria, Guyana, Australia, Syria, Bosnia and El Salvador, and anthologies from Palestine, Cuba, Hungary, Siberia, France, Algeria and the Soviet Union. Three Smokestack books have won PEN Translation awards. Two have been translated into Italian and one into Turkish. Smokestack was recently shortlisted for the Small Press of the Year award.

Smokestack titles are often intended as specific *interventions*, contributions to a conversation about a particular issue – for example, Dinos Siotis (ed) *Crisis* (the Greek economic and political crisis) and Martin Rowson's *Pastrami Faced Racist* (Brexit). A percentage of the sales of Naomi Foyle (ed) *A Blade of Grass: New Palestinian Poetry* goes towards the legal fees of Ashraf Fayadh and Dareen Tatour, Palestinian poets currently imprisoned in Saudi Arabia and Israel on charges relating to their poetry.

This is not, I think, a project entirely lacking in interest, distinction – or radicalism. But of course, no Smokestack title has ever been noticed by the *Guardian*. Only three have ever been reviewed in *Poetry Review*. Smokestack does not receive any public subsidy. This is not a complaint. And it is certainly not a surprise. British literary life has always been an unwelcoming, unfriendly and uncomradely place. There are many reasons why only three Smokestack titles have ever been reviewed in *Poetry Review*, but they have nothing to do with poetry. Anyway, Smokestack was set up in order to oppose the ideological values and cultural assumptions that ignore most poets, most poems and most people most of the time. There are many poetry worlds; the Poetry Society represents just one of them.

Poetry does not need a 'revival' any more than jumping does, or whistling or humming or giggling. Poetry is not cool; it is necessary. It is neither a talent-contest nor an industry. And it has nothing to do with the values of show-business or big-business, corporate PR or copyright law. The importance of poetry is not calculated in sales-figures, and its value is not measured by prizes. Poetry cannot be owned because it already belongs to anyone and everyone.

Among the writers at the al-Marbed festival in Basra was the Iraqi poet Chawki Abdelamir. Stripped of his citizenship in the 1970s, Chawki lived for many years in Algiers, Beirut and Paris (where he was the cultural attaché for the South Yemeni government). He is currently the Iraqi representative on UNESCO. Chawki has translated Guillevic into Arabic, Adonis into French, and published over thirty books, most recently *Attenter à la mort*, which Smokestack is publishing in English next year:

I live in the Baghdad National Library
a blind seer
between lines of ash
I touch the text's carbon
like a child stroking the head
of his dying father

The office chair
is a skeleton with blackened limbs
scrumpling a still white
sheet of paper

From the window
stripped naked by the flames
a dishevelled palm tree stands
reciting hymns
from the index of lost titles
and great chapters of the history of fire
in the parchment of Baghdad

I went out
clutching my pen
like a match

Five Poems

SEAN O'BRIEN

The Party

In the distance there sits the retired volcano
Blowing absent-minded smoke-rings,
Bent to the darkening book of the valley
That tells us its story of panthers and serpents
And roses forever, as if we were children.
Here at the party the beautiful women
Flicker like the long-ago *estrellas*
de ciné, in monochrome Balenciaga,
Almost gone, still smiling on the men
Who will have everything and more,
The horses and the women and the moon
That rises from the dark caldera –
For desire, they will tell you gravely,
Is a duty much like death, its give and take.
Tomorrow is Ash Wednesday. The murderers
Will raise their scythes to join the carnival
Among the floats and masks and children
Dancing to the lakeshore. There at dusk
A coffin will be launched to bear away
The sins that flesh is heir to, free to drift
Until it beaches on the property of those
Who celebrate so grimly here tonight
The beauty of the women they have killed
And mean to kill, and the secret death of politics –
Which is, we learn, another name for sex,
The shallow graves and cellars where the monsters
Swim in blood to be reborn. And somehow
We are here with them, as if we've dreamed
Too long to wake. We ought to go. The horns
Strike up, timbales snap, and the assassins
Take their victims in their arms to make the moves
They've known since they were boys and girls.
It is the custom, and for us to vanish now
Would be discourteous. We join the ring
So smoothly we might be professionals.

An American Activity

For Tamar Yoseloff

As a boy I read the death that Roethke dreamed of:
Running out of road, and then the vehicle stalling
As the windscreen filled with snow.
It stayed with me, that resting-place,
Although in time the car itself became confused
With other wrecks from Dickey and Dave Smith,
Where kudzu coiled like sex among the rusted springs.
Today I find the poem again: now Yeats and Stevens
Look on unamused at Roethke's borrowed robes.
And yet that piety he carried like insurance
To the snowy ditch, to the cliff at world's end,
To the garden men of forty glimpse at dusk
When opening the icebox for the lonely sake of it,
Has never lost its hold. This is their birthright,
Lodged like a minié ball in a skull
At Antietam, a grammar of train-whistles
Heard across the hills a hundred years
And more ago, and never headed here.
Still I am occupied by listening
To a music that can scarcely know itself
And yet meets all occasions: thus they gather at the river,
They return from foreign wars to ignorance and scorn,
They take their turns at parenthood, at burying their own
And at divorce, and – it is evening – come to stand
And watch a baseball diamond left to elegise
Stage four of its neglect, between two railroad yards
While fighting drunks steal bases from their skeletons.
What competence and what complacency:
How inextricable the habit that was there
Before the habits formed, that always knew
A pathway through the woods and past the fatal creek
To find the crazy widow's shotgun shack awaiting
Immortality. The hidden way was marked at every turn,
Secure in all the righteousness that makes
Life look like religion and religion look like them.
These men who at fifty fall for sophomores,
These women who will put themselves to death
In the assault on greatness, cannot be denied
Their place among the saints. As well exclude the air itself
Or dam the smoking waters where they flow
Through burning forests and exhausted plains:
And why should anyone do that, they'd turn and ask,
Supposing they were listening. It is the right of all
To be a headlamp on a northbound train,
Or, lifting up their hearts unto the hills,
To sing of death as if it were a clause
Revoked in secret from the Constitution
And replaced with other words, like these.

Scene of

February. The leaves turn white
from weariness at being dead.

The fences slump on bailer twine.
Fire in an oil drum, purpose unknown.

More birches and more fog
than all the bears in Canada

know what to do with.
To say nothing of the yellow-brown

moquette squalor of indoors,
where nothing works

but repetition: vodka,
smack and child neglect.

The place has spent a lifetime, several,
waiting for its murder.

You could call it a project.
Someone passing through

must grasp its real
potential, and the current

residents, yeah, they want it –
dead, be dead, be done with this.

Give it a week. If they could
ever concentrate they might

be dramatists themselves.
No matter: here it comes.

An Assignation

I will see you in the white square
Once again beneath the plane trees
By the church of St Eulalie.

It will be the middle of the afternoon
When everyone has disappeared
But you and I approaching secretly

By different streets. My life is
Nothing but this rendezvous, my love,
No past, no afterwards, only the breeze

That fidgets like a horse kept waiting
In that distant corner of the square,
Where I can see you now,

Already seated and expecting no one.
Your dress is blue, your book
Lies open by the empty glass you'll raise

As if in toast to no one while I pass
And raise in turn my non-existent hat
In token of this infinite commitment.

Farewell, then. Farewell. À demain.

Wood

But I moot been in prison thurgh Saturne,
And eke thurgh Juno, jalous and eek wood

There are no markers in the woods, the woods themselves
So old, so long sold off into disuse that what appears
To be a woodpile is a drift of fallen birches turning
On the air's slow tide, through which the tide's slow air
Is playing on repeat. This is the wood of the mad
Where under Saturn Palamon would ride,
With its limited palette, grey, brown, grey, grey-white,
Furnished like a secondary hell, its watercourses
Thick with time and halting altogether as they reach
The old sluice at the boundary where all this ends.
The path curves back towards the core, the wood's heart
Neither beating nor unbroken, when the air will pause,
Release itself across the dead white leaves
And having taken stock, cease to be anywhere.

'You Will Know When You Get There'

CHRIS MILLER

Allen Curnow, *Collected Poems*, ed. Elizabeth Caffin and Terry Sturm (AUP) £53.95, 388pp;
Terry Sturm (ed. Linda Cassels), *Allen Curnow. Simply by Sailing in a New Direction. A Biography* (AUP) £62.95, 717pp

A SEVEN HUNDRED-PAGE biography of Allen Curnow? For many Anglophone readers, the first question is: who he? And the *Collected Poems* that accompanies Sturm's life, though it answers this question, is partly supererogatory. The simple answer to the question is that Curnow (1911–2001) was one of the great poets of the twentieth century. But that assertion can be made only about his later work, which barely overlaps with the publication of his first *Collected* in 1974. Curnow's emergence as a poet of international stature began with the publication in 1972 of *Trees, Effigies, Moving Objects* (*TEMO*). Before this date, he had earned a central place in New Zealand poetry as poet, critic and anthologist; his two anthologies of NZ poetry constituted that poetry as literature. His longevity and the poetry of his old age cemented that place so thoroughly that he became a bugbear and inspiration to successive younger generations and his disputatious nature did nothing to pacify the mutineers. Patrick Evans, author of a history of NZ literature, gives a sort of *reductio* of this state of mind. He had criticised Curnow the critic (he is not obviously joking): 'I recall a dream not long after in which I was dragged before him in shackles to explain myself as he sat above me on a massive throne; I remember particularly the slavish quality of my responses.'

Sturm has written a literary biography (he had completed a very extensive full draft when he died in 2009, and this volume was edited to its current dimensions by his wife, Linda Cassels). It is, therefore, the life of the poet rather than the man. The man's life can be briefly told: son of a highly literate clergyman, not expected to go to university, Curnow took up journalism before obtaining a grant to study for the priesthood. The studies opened his eyes to the intellectual and social constraints required for acceptance by the Anglican church and, after seeking a curacy, he gave up on the church and returned to journalism; his services to the *Christchurch Press* were regarded as essential and he therefore played only a home-front-journalist's part in World War II. In 1951, he took a post at Auckland University, which he retained until retirement. His private life was more complicated: he married the artist Betty Le Cren in 1936, had three children, divorced and remarried in 1965. He was survived by his second wife, née Jeny Tole (d. 2013), and Sturm's task was perhaps complicated by this being an 'official' biography. Sturm refers obliquely to Curnow's infidelities to Betty but we hear mainly of those that left a record in his poetry. Yet he also notes that Curnow had been secretly involved with Jeny for seven years before his divorce, and when he describes this as 'a remarkable love story', one doubts that this would be Betty's qualification. That duplicity was obviously a very important fact in Curnow's life and one of the factors contributing to *TEMO*, the 'breakout' volume of 1974.

The breakout consisted of bringing the full armoury of Modernism to bear on religious belief, patriotism and notions of human progress. It is a bitter liberation, in which the former theology student and the literary scholar both play a role alongside the expatriate and the urban and littoral dog-walker; the ceremonies of innocence are vitiated, monuments serve only to justify exceptionalism, and the tree of knowledge has become 'an iron receptacle'. Over this and subsequent volumes, moreover, the threat of nuclear annihilation hangs (I think there is no other poetic corpus in which the nuclear threat of the Cold War is registered with such experiential conviction). But *TEMO* is also, I think, a document about the anger of a man who, in middle age, finds the love of his life, cannot openly declare the fact without losing his job (teaching jobs, Sturm says, required an unblemished marital record and Jeny too was a teacher) and is forced to conceal his love on monetary grounds. An equivalent attack on human consolations might be Geoffrey Hill's *King Log*. But there is room, still, for a sort of secular contentment in the theological vacuum: 'There is standing room and much to be thankful for / in the present. Look, a dead lamb on the beach.'

TEMO marked the end of a ten-year poetic silence. Curnow's earliest poems had come out of his spiritual crisis but by his second book, *Enemies* (1937), he had turned spiritual critic of NZ society. By *Island and Time* (1941), he was at his most Audenesque and portentous, engaging in a kind of public metaphysics: 'Man, his hour, his marvellous thought descend / Through perpetual beginning and perpetual end.' *Sailing or Drowning* (1943) includes the public poetry of 'Landfall in Unknown Seas', which, in combination with Douglas Lilburn's music, became a kind of NZ calling card, alongside other definitive statements of the Zeitgeist, such as 'The Skeleton of the Great Moa in the Canterbury Museum, Christchurch': 'Not I, some child, born in a marvellous year, / Will learn the trick of standing upright here.' When Curnow was finally able to travel in 1949, his horizons expanded: *At Dead Low Water* (1949) recalls epoch-making events: Dylan Thomas, whom he had just met, echoes through 'Elegy on My Father' and 'When the Hulk of the World', while elegies to Thomas and Wallace Stevens rather nakedly bear the impress of their style. Though the seeds of Curnow's later themes are present, his diction still shifted among wide-ranging influences.

The working-out of the 'matter of NZ' was becoming clearer in that and the two subsequent volumes, as Curnow's interests took a more metaphysical turn, relating now to Descartes and phenomenalism rather than to religion or its social implications. That working-out had also been accomplished in his famous anthologies, 1945 and 1960, and their introductions, some of whose phrases left a permanent mark on NZ poetics:

> The idea that we are confronted by a natural time, a natural order, to which our presence in these islands is accidental, irrelevant; that we are interlopers on an indifferent or hostile scene; that idea, or misgiving, occurs so variously and so often, and in the work of New Zealand poets otherwise so different, that it suggests some common problem of the imagination.

And, most famously of all, 'Reality must be local and special at the point where we pick up the traces... Whatever is true vision belongs, here, uniquely to the island of New Zealand' (1960). He was accused of propagating regionalism and a South Island myth. The later anthology was ready for the press by late 1956, and was delayed by the objections of certain of the poets, notably Eileen Duggan, Louis Johnson and James K. Baxter. Duggan had demanded control of what the editor said about her and was excised. Johnson and Baxter contrived to have a sight of the introduction and refused their permissions; they were eventually won over by Penguin but this quarrel laid the grounds for long drawn-out hostilities. Curnow had little use for the olive branch, and, having made special efforts to include Baxter's debuts in his first anthology, was legitimately affronted when Baxter impugned his qualifications as an anthologist to the London publisher. By the early 1970s, all this mattered less. Curnow was happily remarried, had travelled again to the United States, where his lectures and poems were admired, and was not far from retirement. It was, clearly, a good time to begin his poetic career all over again.

This he certainly did. In collections prior to this posthumous volume, Curnow makes this clear. *Continuum: New and Later Poems* (1988) contains all his volumes back to *TEMO* in reverse chronological order, as if to mark the watershed; the Penguin *Selected Poems 1940–1989* (1990) includes all of *Continuum* and selections from his earlier work; Carcanet's *Early Days Yet: New and Collected Poems 1941–1997* (1997) gave pre-1972 material just sixty-two pages in two hundred and thirty-nine pages of poems. Curnow's second book after *TEMO*, *An Incorrigible Music* (1979) is a consummate performance: an account of humanity as 'killers by necessity'. It conflates fishing from the Cathedral Rock at Karekare with the Pazzi conspiracy to murder Ludovico and Giuliano de' Medici in the Florence Duomo. Some critics found the savage relish of the book masterful but repellent. With *TEMO*, this and the two books that followed – *You Will Know When You Get There* (1982) and *The Loop in Lone Kauri Road* (1986) – constitute Curnow's principal claims to major status. They are very hard to describe. I have offered the term 'post-modern metaphysical'; they focus consistently on the process and subjectivity of perception and are informed with a sense of Curnow's own mortality, which is several times rehearsed. The two later books centre on the landscape of the Curnows' hometown, Auckland, and the littoral of their 'bach' at Karekare. They combine Cartesian metaphysics and an awareness of literary theory with something like solipsism. Curnow's 'attempts' are 'always analytic'; there is 'a direct sensuous apprehension of thought, or a recreation of thought into feeling' (Eliot). Here is late Curnow at his humorous best, in 'Canto of Signs without Wonders' from *The Loop*:

> I look where I'm going, it's the way
>   yesterday's and the day before's clouds
>   depict themselves over and over
>
> an affluently planted skyline:
>   the clouds lay the whitenesses on thick
>   over the bluenesses. The impasto
>
> is unsigned, there's a kind of impression
>   of lettering rapidly rubbed out
>   before I can read, pasted over again
>
> and rewritten, the name of a famous
>   product, the thing that's everything,
>   the sky being prime space, anyway

No one else writes like this. If you haven't read late Curnow, the volumes cited above, *Continuum* and *Early Days Yet*, are the places to start; if you began with Curnow's earliest work in this *Collected*, you would very likely be discouraged before reaching a poem that I could recommend.

Sturm is an excellent critic and unfailingly lucid; the biography is best read as an extended and indispensable commentary on Curnow's entire works, drafted, published and collected. In the *Collected Poems*, the reader is assisted by an online archive, which contains poems published but uncollected alongside two satirical broadsheets and the original published text of the three early volumes that Curnow revised for the 1974 collected poems. The existence of the Appendix might seem to define the nature of the *Collected*, limiting it to poems that the poet collected during his lifetime in the form of his final published revisions. It is therefore exceptionable to find that, in the section 'Poems from the 1960s', Caffin has included three unpublished poems, one of which draws on a page 'heavily altered by hand and... not altogether clear'. The introduction blandly remarks: 'I have also included an interesting group of poems from the 1960s partly on the grounds of their literary merit but also to show that though no major collection appeared in these years, the poet was not idle'. The decade of silence between *A Small Room with Large Windows* (1962) and *TEMO* was indeed one that Curnow resented and even attempted to paper over; but it is no part of an editor's remit to pander to this and we note that Curnow himself refrained from publishing these poems. It is even more astonishing to find a satirical broadsheet here, when the two others are in the Appendix. Curnow had a popular, well-remunerated heteronym, Whim-Wham, who wrote light, topical verse for a newspaper column and he took pains never to confuse Whim-Wham's verse-journalism with Curnow's poetry. Caffin should have followed this line; none of the broadsheets were signed by Whim-Wham but the appendix would have made this one available without confusing genres. Two previously uncollected poems published in anthologies are also included. Why? The notes to the *Collected Poems* are described as 'extensive' but do not identify all the quotations with which Curnow studded his poetry – indeed, for this the biography is a better bet. I miss the exemplary organisation found in Share's *The Poems of Basil Bunting,* in which at the bottom of each page of notes are the corresponding page numbers of the poetry. The *Collected* is a handsome volume on excellent paper but not beyond criticism.

The biography is a considerable achievement: meticulous, compendious and immensely well informed. It is extremely circumstantial: Sturm benefited from his early interest in Curnow and the preservation of much of his correspondence. He has chosen from this with fine tact and his account inspires almost complete trust. Seven hundred pages may seem daunting for a relatively unadventurous life but much of it is taken up with analysing and commenting on Curnow's poetry and criticism. Do we need to know which poems Curnow read at the many readings of his later life? Perhaps we do; it casts a certain light on his own sense of his work. But this biography completely fails to account for the strong dislike that Curnow inspired in some of those who came into contact with him. The Shirley Horrocks documentary, also called *Early Days Yet* (available online at 'NZ on Screen'), shows a rather lovable nonagenarian. But in Vincent O'Sullivan's poem 'Art and Life, say', a group of intellectuals give a 'not-long-dead-poet' 'unstinted credit' for his 'faultless pitch / and a savage toughness of mind'. If the living poet had walked in, however, they'd all be 'off like a shot'. This is the Curnow missing from Sturm's biography and I, who met and was charmed by the man, would like to know a little more about him. The poetry will survive such discoveries.

Three Poems

Lisa Kelly

Ossuary

Arrête! C'est ici l'empire de la Mort

In the queue for the Catacombs only the cold
and cursing the kids for cajoling me into this
is keeping the contents of my guts from spilling.
Behind, two German teenagers cram croissants
into their mouths, and ahead the undead
count out coins for entry into the underworld,
one-at-a-tortuous time down the spiral stairwell
we will eventually reach, just as I will eventually
retch in my hotel bathroom.

For now, I contemplate this world of stone and bone,
the colour of maggots, relieved only by green mould
on a stacked skull. I know I can spill my guts later,
not down here with the crosses and inscriptions,
so long as I keep walking, the putting of one foot in front
of another taking on the pace of prayer – a prayer
for escape my mother-in-law didn't share, happy
to hear sirens and clasp her classmates in the shelter
of the grave, *not just with the skulls*, as she said,
but with the tibia and fibula, swapping one lesson
in biology for another as the bombs dropped
and created a longer queue for a burial chamber.

The Haute Schiaparelli

Hold onto your shoe hat cowgirl, we're in for a bumpy ride
when Elsa scents her spray. 'Light the way to ecstasy',
the strapline for *Sleeping* bottled in a crystal candlestick.

Our Elsa had wild ideas and was not one to be tamed.
Cattle Empires, Fashion Empires; all so much meat to the bone.
Take your shining apex of an idea and corral it girlfriend.

You did that darling with *Le Roy Soleil*, a Baccarat bottle
designed by Dali to celebrate the end of World War II
with a Surrealist gold sun stopper, enthroned on a glass ocean.

But every high noon has a Skeleton Evening Dress
hanging in the closet; a Lobster Dinner Dress poised to pinch;
a veiled Tears Dress to reveal the shadow of a showdown.

The Naked Lady

Her bronze body, sculpted by Guillaume, stands sixteen feet high.
She is known – affectionately – as Dirty Gertie.

Her bronze body, sculpted by Guillaume, stands sixteen feet high,
resolute as cars on Regents Park Road speed by.
Many a troubadour in North Circular territory
has courted her with a *cobla esparsa* composed on the fly
over and over, her uncovered sword pierces the sky.
Her story of unveiling was in no way flirty.
Lloyd George said *La Délivrance* was a symbol of victory
in a war which delivered us from the despot's eye.
The newsflash did not flesh out her nudity.
In the 1920 Paris Salon, she made a newspaper magnate shy.
She is known – affectionately – as Dirty Gertie.

Thoughts

Andrew Wynn Owen

i. The Task

Mapmakers? No, more like composers, setting
desire in step with speech,
constructing, channelling, begetting
what once seemed out of reach:
the peaceful intra-variance of things,
a net that nature cast to teach
attentive senses. Tangled ivy slings
organic links
along a wall. Time flings
its fractious brinks
and hectic brevities against
the baffled sphinx
of pattern-spattered truth, sought for and sensed.

ii. Stuff

Widgity bugs, shoe trees, and jellied eels.
all these and so much more.
Whatever gives your gut the feels.
there's all of it in store.
Roof shingles, washing lines, and vintage vinyl.
Fast liver, pause and, I implore,
Perceive it all, its strangeness. Ah, your spine'll
tingle, shiver,
and none of this is final.
incessant river!
Trim dendrites of the psyche quickly
cluster and quiver.
Red roses fascinate, though oh-so-prickly.

iii. Against the Ironists (1)

It bites, but where's the nuzzling kiss? Too often,
lost spirits, in a mood,
go brittle when they ought to soften.
Who spits the meat they've chewed?
Who salts the sore when they should bring the plaster?
Who never, dazzled, dumbstruck, viewed
A landscape loving hands took pains to master,
with wild delight?
Who titters at disaster
and 'Some day might
attempt a novel'? Ironists,
who meet this bright
receptive world with smirks and ready fists.

iv. Afterlife

Tear ducts can go three days without cessation,
but everything runs out,
even the art of contemplation.
Chin up: resist the rout,
and plot a course for hope, that fissile zone,
home of the dreamer's roundabout
approaches to euphoria's furious throne.
It is a rage
for worlds we cannot own:
a mutant stage,
a plectrum-pluck from faraway
that awes our age
and drives us, though defiant, till life's last day

when speech will, in a trice, become absurd.
Until that hour, however,
we live to phoenix, fix, the word
in scorched arrangements, ever
reallocating all that's been allowed
by ravenous nature. That endeavour
is our torrential reckoning with a cloud
of blank unknowing,
through which we slip the crowd
and keep thought flowing.
How else should we know when to halt
or where we're going?
Tumultuous effort, but a real result.

v. *Youth* (2015)

In Sorrentino's latest, *Giovinezza*,
the composer's daughter gets
jilted abruptly in the mezzo-
giorno of life. Regrets
and tears abound. Perhaps the cruellest blow
is when the other woman jets
on screen and, with disgust, we come to know
she's a pop star.
can you relate? I'd go,
for now, so far
as to suggest that, in these tame
times, avatar
of shrugged-off dreams, a poet feels the same.

VI. AGAINST THE IRONISTS (2)

Blood on their pens. Warmonger's guilt for all
who snipe that hope can't matter;
who, flummoxed, wish the rest to fall;
who, grizzly, grinchy, clatter
through galleries inspecting specks of dust.
Nit-picking wind and water batter
sea-cliffs to circulate debris, but must
these cynics dredge
life's slurry, showcase rust?
I cannot hedge
my horror of them, hearts so frozen,
who never pledge;
whose only Eros is their god Erosion.

VII. A SCALE OF GRIEF
after Don Paterson

Richter and Beaufort christened crisis scales.
I etched mine on my wrist:
One. When all previous feeling fails;
Two. When defeat's fast fist
is nothing to your gut's sad turbulence;
Three. When you turn anthologist
for shiver, sayonara, jumbled tense,
a bleary sun
exploding commonsense
by megaton.
Pales to: Ten. Ruining poetry
for everyone.
(Not work, this knotwork. Grief's last ditch for play.)

VIII. EKSTASIS

Occasionally it gets you and you go
wild, wordless, wonderstruck.
With distance, yes, it is de trop,
but, in the flow, your luck
feels difficult to fathom, doubt and cloud
dispelled to let you run amuck
in flawless exultation, tension, wowed
as everything
declares its name in loud
heart-staggering
seraphic letters. High and low,
love's vanishing
no longer bothers. All is well, you know?

IX. DE BRUIJN

De Bruijn: combinatoric prompt for these
gear-changing speculations.
But to what end? To teach and tease;
the gaiety of nations;
exactitude of cerebellum-work,
perception-sharpening. Cogitations
intended to array the land of quirk
in freedom's cause,
which, in this wordy work,
permits no pause
from operating on the spine
of natural laws.
One slip-up – you send shivers down the line.

From the Archive

Issue 147, September–October 2002

ROBERT MINHINNICK

From 'Cefn Hirgoed', a long poem of eleven sequences, subtitled 'In the Fever Hospital'. Fellow contributors to this issue include Carola Luther, Sinéad Morrisey, Marilyn Hacker, Jeremy Over, Geoffrey Hill and John Ashbery.

from CEFN HIRGOED

I come out of the wood
with my head on fire

And my mother places her nurse's hand upon
my brow
and my father sits me down in the rocking chair

And asks, did you see the animals,
did you see the animals?

But all I know is the sunlight
is already turning to ashes in my head

And there is a steel reinforcing rod
pushing through the hollow of my spine

And I cannot speak
so they put me in a room behind a glass wall

[...]

A New Divan

A Lyrical Dialogue between East & West

ABBAS BEYDOUN

Suleika and Marilyn

English version by Bill Manhire, based on a literal translation from the Arabic by Reem Ghanayem

من قلب البئر صعد صوتي، والذئب الّذي إخترعوه لي، سمعني وهرب
القميص الّذي بللوه بدم كاذب أعشى عيني أبي
هل كان البئر حقيقيّا، هل كان القميص حقيقيا؟
هل صدقت الصحراء، هل صدق الذّئب؟
ما الّذي كان ينتظرني عند فم البئر؟
سوى طريق الأنبياء إلى مصر

في كتاب قديم وجدت أنا الشاعر بلاطا و ملكة وسجنا
الجميلة الّتي أحبّت يوسف قطعت أصابعها من أجله
ليس أقلّ من دم حقيقي هذه المرّة، ليس أقلّ من قميص حقيقي
أنا الشاعر لا أجد دما لقصيدتي، بريت أصابعي لأكتبها
وجدت زليخا في مخيّم للنازحين تحمل مكواة حامية
أحرقت أصابعها وقرّحتها
صورة أخيها الميّت معلّقة على الحائط
أنا الشاعر أعرف أنّها نزفت من يديها، وهي تجلي، فوق الصحون
أن جمالها مطموس في أسمالها

أفكّر الآن بمارلين مونرو الّتي إنتحرت من شقاء العالم
وصعوبة الحبّ
لقد أشرقت على ملايين غادروا الصالات وإنصرفوا إلى أعمالهم
قالوا أنّها مختلّة، إنتظروا جميعا أن تنضج لتستحقّهم

أنا الشاعر، أعرف أنّي لست كحافظ ولا سعدي ولا المتنبي ولا جلال الدّين الرومي
اولئك تطلّعوا إلى ما يجعلهم أعلى من أنفسهم، إلى تجربة كونيّة
كانوا يتّصلون بالكون عن طريق الحب، كانوا يسمعون النجوم عن طريق الحب
الشعراء اليوم مساجين في غرف الآلات
هم وحدهم ونساؤهم من ورق
العالم ينتكس، وأنفسنا تنتكس معه، إنّها تنظر فقط إلى ما هو أدنى منها
ثمنها الوحيد هو الموت، الإنتحار من أجل لا شيء، في عالم لم يعد له سعر
زليخا في البلاط إنتظرت شيئا أعلى من تاج، شيئا أكثر من ملك
الجمال السماوي الّذي جاء من بئر في الصحراء كان أصيلا وكونيّا
يوسف الّذي لم يأكله الذّئب ولا الصحراء رأى ما وراء النجوم
زليخا بأصابعها المقطوعة، المزهرة والمضيئة، لامست السماء

ماذا تفعل أيّها الشاعر العجوز، أنت الّذي لا يقطفك أحد
حتّى متى تنتظر زليخا
لقد واكبت مارلين إلى القبر
وعمّا قريب في مكان آخر ستقع في الحفرة
بدون هدف، ولن يخرجك أحد من البئر
إنّه موعدك مع اللاأحد

I heard myself call from deep in the well.
The wolf my brothers invented, he listened and fled.
It wasn't my blood on the shirt, but still our father was blinded.
Was there a real well? A real shirt?
Was the desert a true place? Was the wolf himself actual?
What awaited me up on the earth's surface
but the Prophets' Road to Egypt?

In an ancient book
I found a court, a queen, a keep.
Suleika loved Yusuf and cut her fingers...
Oh, real blood that time; a real shirt, too.

I am searching for blood for my poem.
My fingers grow sharp as I write it.
I find Suleika in a refugee camp.
The hot iron she carries
burns and blisters her fingers.
On the wall, a photo of her dead brother;
I can see how her hands bleed as she does the dishes,
how her beauty is there in the rags she wears.

And now I am thinking of Marilyn Monroe.
She took her life because the world is made of pain
plus tiny scraps of love. She shone high on the screen
and a million men returned to their lives. Ah, they said,
is she quite stable? One day she will surely grow up
and acknowledge our worth!

I am just a little voice. Hafiz, Saadi, Rumi, Mutanabbi...
they sang beyond themselves, their embrace went wide.
Love held them up to the universe,
they listened to the stars. These days
poets are locked in their machines,
each one alone with a woman made of paper.
Ours is an age that drifts and slides, and we go with it;
we seek small things that never mattered,
find suicide and death in a world without worth.
Suleika waited for more than a crown, a king.
True divinity came from that well in the desert.
Yusuf, who survived the wolf, saw beyond the stars.
Suleika's fingers flowered and flamed and touched the sky.

And you, what will you do, old fellow, old poet,
you whom no one has use for?
How long must Suleika wait?
Marilyn moves towards her grave.
Soon and in another place you will plunge
deep into the earth and thus beyond all purpose,
and no one there to lift you back to the surface.
Oh this is your date with no one.

MOHAMMED BENNIS

Aubade

English version by Sinéad Morrissey,
based on a literal translation from the Arabic by Mbarek Sryfi

يا سيّدَ الشُّعراءِ غُوتَه
غنّيْتُ من أدْنَى بلادِ الشرْقِ كأساً كنتَ تشْربُها سعيداً
تحتَ داليةٍ وتعْرفُ أنها خيْرٌ تماماً كلُّها

وحْدي هُنا في حَانةِ الغُرباءِ يمْلأُ كأْسيَ السّاقي
نبيذاً صافياً
كأساً تلي كأساً
وفي سرِّي أبارِكُ نشْوَةً
مُتنسّكاً أتعلّمُ الغرْبَ الذي أوْدعتَهُ في جوْهرِ الكلماتِ

أنتَ أَنا
أراكَ اليوْمَ من زَمنٍ إلى زَمنٍ تعودُ
تُطلُّ منْ معْراجكَ الكوْنيِّ يجْمعُ بيْنـنَا حُلمٌ
تكوّنَ منْ مدَادِكَ عندمَا سُكرٌ
وشطْحٌ فيكَ ظلاّ طائريْن إلى الأعَالي شُعلةً يتلألآنْ

حقّاً سأرْفعُ ضوْءَ كأسكَ
لا سبيلَ سواهُ في زمني الجَريحِ كأنما شوقٌ إليْكَ يقودُ
من غرْبٍ إلى شرقٍ يدُورُ الكأسُ لي سُكْرٌ
يُمجّدُ ما يديمُ عليَّ أنْ أحْيا بعيداً عنْ غباءِ الحقْدِ

أعرفُ أن وقتَ الضّيْق صارَ اليوْمَ أعْتَى
باسْم مَا سمّوْهُ شرْعيةً
ولكنّي بماءِ الحُبّ أغسلُ ما تدنّسَ في النّفوسْ

أهْلاً بكأسٍ منْ نبيـذٍ يُشبه الياقُوتْ
سأشربُ في مديحِ العشْقِ هذا الكأسَ ليْلاً ثم ليْلاً
سوْفَ أسْعَى مُخْلصاً لنشيدِ منْ غنّى
منَ الشعراءِ للأرضِ التي تبقَى
لنَا أُمّاً كما كانتْ

أنَا السّكرانُ
أبصرُ آيةَ المجْهولِ مُشرقةً
على صمْتٍ توحّدَ بي
وفـيّاً لانْفتاحِ اللاّنهايةِ بيْننا
فرَحاً به أبداً أكونْ

O Goethe Master of Poets
from the most Westerly land of the East have I sung in praise
of the glass you raised to happiness under a grapevine
and saw goodness in all things blossom

Alone at the bar, strangers everywhere,
the waiter is filling my glass with wine
glass after glass
and I bless this inner welling bliss
which shows me the West, the West you distilled to its literal essence

You have become me –
Today I see you, flickering revenant,
looking down at me from the whirl of your ascension
the two of us bound by the self-same dream,
together entranced by the spell your ink cast
when waywardness and drunkenness remained steadfast
sparks flying upwards

Yes, I'll raise your light-filled glass
These damaged days, I have no other choice but this
as if my thirst to be one with you could set down a path
from West to East place in my hands the intoxicating glass
carry me far from the stupidity of hate
glorify everything that makes me carry on living

In this time of hardship, truth bickered over by despots,
with the water of love shall I wash the soul
clean of all profanity

So welcome, glass of ruby-jewelled wine!
From this glass will I drink in praise of love
night after night will I faithfully strive
to praise those amongst the host of poets
who sang for the land – as it once was and ever shall be –
the poets' mother country

I, the drunk –
I see the wondrous unknown shining
on a silence that cocks its head and beckons
In the spaces between us, infinity opens
This my faith, this my happiness

The poems 'Suleika and Marilyn' and 'Aubade' are taken from A New Divan: A Lyrical Dialogue between East & West *published by Gingko (forthcoming June 2019).*

Exile: Part III

André Naffis-Sahely

ALTHOUGH IT TOOK only twenty years for Poland to be partitioned, it would require over one hundred and twenty years to be put back together.* As the translator Boris Dralyuk has noted, the result of those invasions was that 'the story of modern Polish literature to a large extent' became 'a story of exile' and that while Poland died as a political entity, it survived in the works of Adam Mickiewicz (1798–1855) who was born in what became Russian Lithuania in the year of the Third Partition and who died in Constantinople in 1855. A poem penned by Mickiewicz in either 1839 or 1840, but never published, shows him having grown listless to his surroundings, after long, peripatetic years in Russia, Germany, Italy, Switzerland and France, nevertheless retaining a hold on the spiritual Poland in his heart: 'I have a country, homeland of my thoughts, / where my heart has innumerable kin: / a land more fair than what I see before me, / a family more dear than anything.'

Going by Newton's Third Law, it is little wonder that the Age of Nations would produce the internationalist socialist movement, and it is even less surprising that the cosmopolitan component of that progressive ideology would attract the spleen of patriots and jingoists everywhere. On 11 July 1917, executives of the Phelps Dodge corporation, which ran the copper mines and border town of Bisbee, Arizona, like a medieval fief, colluded with Harry Wheeler, the local sheriff, to deport over a thousand miners who had been on a peaceful week-long strike for better working conditions. Many of the strikers belonged to the Industrial Workers of the World (IWW). Bolshevik-inspired paranoia was in the air and, facing a sharp drop in copper prices, Phelps Dodge executives decided to break the strike by any means necessary. Their plan was ruthlessly ambitious: roughly an eighth of Bisbee's population was to be exiled in a single morning. In order to arrange this mammoth expulsion, the sheriff deputised two thousand local gunmen from the surrounding areas of Cochise County, gave them white armbands and weapons and unleashed them on the unsuspecting miners. The El Paso and Southwestern Railroad provided a dozen cattle cars for the operation, and following six hours of mayhem, from early morning to noon, 1,186 men, women and children were loaded onto trains under armed guard and sent to Hermanas, New Mexico, two hundred miles to the east.

None of those involved in the Bisbee Deportation of 1917 were ever imprisoned for their actions, and Phelps Dodge's rule over Bisbee actually tightened. Deportees who returned were denied work, while the unions were effectively shut out of mining operations. Further underscoring the company's influence, all talk of the deportation was squashed until the 1980s, when most mining operations ceased. Fortunately, however, a poem survives. It was published in the IWW's *One Big Union Monthly* in August 1919: 'We are waiting, brother, waiting / Tho the night be dark and long' the poem begins, before detailing the experience of that terrible day, 'we were herded into cars / And it seemed our lungs were bursting / With the odor of the Yards. / Floors were inches deep in refuse / Left there from the Western herds. / Good enough for miners. Damn them. / May they soon be food for birds'. The poem was unsigned, the only indication to the author's identity was his union card number, 512210.

A mere two years following the Deportation, the same violent hysteria led to Emma Goldman's banishment to Russia aboard the USS *Buford* on 21 December 1919. Like the Bisbee strikers, Goldman had dared to question the validity of the American Dream, and despite her thirty-four years in the US, her belief that the Dream was nothing more than a pyramid scheme made it clear that she was still a foreigner. The supposed foreignness of Goldman's political beliefs therefore came to justify, in the eyes of American conservatives, her denaturalisation and exile. Indeed, although American nativists accused progressives and proponents of social and economic reform of being dangerous foreigners out to destroy America's uniqueness, it was overwhelmingly clear to observers like Goldman that by so doing, America was becoming as tyrannical as the rest of the world:

> I looked at my watch. It was 4:20 a.m. on the day of our Lord, December 21, 1919. On the deck above us I could hear the men tramping up and down in the wintry blast. I felt dizzy, visioning a transport of politicals doomed to Siberia, the *étape* of former Russian days. Russia of the past rose before me and I saw the revolutionary martyrs being driven into exile. But no, it was New York, it was America, the land of liberty! Through the port-hole I could see the great city receding into the distance, its sky-line of buildings traceable by their rearing heads. It was my beloved city, the metropolis of the New World. It was America, indeed, America repeating the terrible scenes of tsarist Russia! I glanced up — the Statue of Liberty!

The sad fates of Nicola Sacco (1891–1921) and Bartolomeo Vanzetti (1888–1921), two working-class immigrant anarchists who were wrongfully convicted of violent armed robbery due to their unpopular political beliefs, were eulogised by the Filipino-American writer and labour activist Carlos Bulosan (1913–56) in his poem 'American History', which fashions the final scene of both men's lives into a haunting portrait as Vanzetti, 'the dreamy fish-peddler' and Sacco, 'the good shoemaker', dream of a 'future that never was', 'in spheres of tragic light, dreaming of the world / that never was, as each tragic moment passed / in streams of vivid light, to radiate a harmony / of thought and action that never came to pass'.

*

* This occurred after World War I.

Oppression at home usually paled in comparison to oppression abroad, and the stories and novels of the Italo-Syro-Libyan Alessandro Spina, né Basili Shafik Khouzam (1927–2013), are fuelled by the intensity of the horrors of the Italian colonial experience in Libya. In 1939, when Spina was twelve, Italy officially annexed Libya, by which time Italian settlers constituted twelve percent of the population and over a third of the inhabitants of Tripoli and Benghazi, the epicentres of Italian power. Nevertheless, what had been expected to be an easy conquest in 1911 had instead turned into a twenty-year insurgency that was quelled only when the Fascists took power in Rome and Mussolini, in a quest to solve Italy's emigration problem, dispatched one of his most ruthless generals, the hated Rodolfo Graziani (1882–1955), to bring the *quarta sponda* (fourth shore) to heel and 'make room' for colonists. Genocide ensued: a third of Libya's population was killed; tens of thousands were interned in concentration camps; a three-hundred-kilometre barbed-wire fence was erected on the Egyptian border to block rebels from receiving supplies and reinforcements; and the leader of the resistance, a venerable Koranic teacher named Omar Mukhtar (1858–1931), was hunted down and summarily hanged.

Alessandro Spina's 'The Fort at Régima', is set in the mid-1930s, when an Italian officer, Captain Valentini, is ordered south of Benghazi to take command of a garrison stationed in an old Ottoman fortress that 'recalled the castles built in Greece by knights who had joined the Fourth Crusade'. Valentini is glad to leave Benghazi and its tiresome military parades behind, but as he's driven to his new posting, his mind is suddenly flooded with the names of famous Crusaders who had 'conquered Constantinople, made and unmade Emperors, carved the vast Empire into fiefs, and run to and fro vainly fighting to ensure the survival of a system, which owing to its lack of roots in the country, was never destined to survive'. Employing only a few hundred words, Spina slices across seven hundred years, showing the inanity of the concept of conquest as well as the existential vacuum it inevitably leaves in its wake: 'As he weltered about in his armoured vehicle, it seemed cruel to the Captain to be forced to undergo the same rigmarole after so many centuries had passed.'

As the Peruvian journalist José Carlos Mariátegui (1894–1930) noted, while Leon Trotsky was well known as one of the chief engineers of the Soviet takeover of Russia, he was above all 'a man of the cosmopolis' and that as such, his exile from Russia had been inevitable: 'The Russian revolution is in a period of national organization.' Mariátegui noted:

> It is not a matter, at the moment, of establishing socialism internationally, but of realising it in a nation that, while a nation of 130 million inhabitants that overflows onto two continents, does not yet constitute a geographical and historical unit. It is logical that in this stage, the Russian revolution is represented by men who more deeply sense its national character and problems. Stalin, a pure Slav, is one of these men. He belongs to a phalanx of revolutionaries who always remained rooted in the Russian soil, while Trotsky, Radek, and Rakovsky belong to a phalanx that passed the larger part of their lives in exile. They were apprenticed as international revolutionaries in exile, an apprenticeship that has given the Russian revolution its universalist language and its ecumenical vision. For now, alone with its problems, Russia prefers more simply and purely Russian men.

As the translator Stephen Kessler has noted, 'the murder of Lorca and the scattering of others into exile or into the mountains to defend the Republic against Francisco Franco's fascist invaders was a cultural cataclysm to match the political and military catastrophe of the next three years – a catastrophe that turned into the protracted nightmare of a four-decades-long dictatorship'. In 1938, when things were looking especially bleak in Spain, Luis Cernuda (1902–63) accepted an invitation to lecture in London and never returned. He taught there and in Glasgow, Scotland, until 1947 when he accepted a position at Mount Holyoke – a women's college where he wouldn't even have the invigorating experience of lusting after his students. Openly homosexual in his life and his writing, Cernuda chronicled his misery during these years of exile in the North even as he continued to create some of his best poems and to establish himself as one of his generation's most astute and respected critics. Arguably one of the most famous of the Spanish Generation of '27 poets', Cernuda's 'Impression of Exile', most likely written either in 1939 or 1940, finds the poet mingling with a crowd in the 'salon of the old Temple, in London' and suddenly overhearing , 'From someone's lips', 'Heavy as a falling teardrop', the single word 'Spain', which carries with it all the emotional burdens of the Republic's downfall and the permanent loss of his motherland, given that Cernuda would die in exile twelve years before the demise of Francisco Franco (1892–1975).

Although the Russian poet Elena Shvarts (1948–2010) is now generally considered among her generation's most important, her translator Sasha Dugdale noted that 'she was not adequately recognised in Russia' and that while she 'received more critical attention and admiration elsewhere, like many unofficial Soviet poets, she was denied the opportunity to travel abroad until 1989'. Shvarts's essay 'Why, Let the Stricken Deer Go Weep' is about her mother, Dina, who studied at the Leningrad Theatre Institute during World War II and the infamous Siege of Leningrad, and who was evacuated in 1942 to Pyatigorsk. As the essay begins, the Germans have advanced so rapidly that the soldiers and the town's administration all flee again, this time south to Tbilisi. 'While Shvarts barely sketches the scene,' Dugdale elucidated:

> any Russian reader would understand immediately the contrast between starving Leningrad and the beautiful southern spa town of Pyatigorsk, where the poet Lermontov was killed in a duel, with its mountain air, mineral springs and sanatoriums, which were operating as war hospitals until the German invasion in August 1942. When the Germans invade Pyatigorsk, not everyone leaves. With our gift of hindsight, the reluctance to flee may seem suicidal, but if you consider the suffering and fearful confusion that was Soviet Russia at the time, German occupation and staying put may have seemed the lesser of a number of evils. Radlov's decision to remain, and his tour of Hamlet in Germany, is a curious legend which I first heard quite recently from the theatre

critic, Alyona Karas. Shvarts maintains that Radlov chose not to evacuate his theatre south to Tbilisi when the Germans approached. I have read elsewhere that the theatre troupe left and Radlov and his wife remained. Other versions of the story describe how Radlov simply did not manage to evacuate his theatre from Pyatigorsk in time. But all seem to agree on the fact that Radlov's theatre was moved by the Germans to Zaporozhe, where the theatre premiered Hamlet, and then, in September 1943, to Berlin. Part of the theatre subsequently went to France, where it performed Ostrovskii's *Guilty Without Guilt*: an example of rarely bettered theatrical irony.

*

Since the downfall of the Ottoman Empire and the Balfour Declaration, the Middle East's near-continuous defragmentation over the past century has ensured its writers have endured violent retaliations against their work in a way perhaps almost entirely unknown in most other parts of the world. Naguib Mahfouz (1911–2006) was stabbed in the neck, the Palestinian writer Ghassan al-Kanafani (1936–72) was murdered by the Mossad, the Egyptian intellectual Nawal El Saadawi (1931–) has lived under police protection, Kateb Yacine (1929–89) was sent into internal exile, while the great Abdulrahman Munif (1933–2004) was stripped of his Saudi citizenship and forced to live in exile in Syria. At the age of seven, Mahmoud Darwish's (1941–2008) native village of al-Birwa in Galilee was razed to the ground, forever shaping the identity of the poet who would become the voice of Palestinians in exile and one of the most famous poets in the world. Although Darwish's compatriot Edward Said (1935–2003) considered exile an 'unhealable rift', a loss that would permanently undermine all achievements in its wake, Darwish took a very different view, which he arguably elaborated best in his prose book, *In The Presence of Absence*, which he wrote only two years prior to his untimely death:

> Exile is not journeying, it is not moving back and forth. Nor is it to dwell in longing. It may be a visit, or a waiting room – what time does to you, or a departure of the self for another, to know and be in harmony with, or for the self to return to its skin. Each exile has its character and every exile his characteristics. In exile you train yourself to contemplate and admire what is not yours.

*

As technological advancement shortened distances, economic migration accordingly increased, and in a time of renewed xenophobia, as the West raises its drawbridge to keep out the rabble spilling from its past and present colonies, many would benefit from turning to the words of Mary Antin (1881–1949), a Jew who emigrated from Czarist Russia at the age of ten and who twenty years later penned a famous memoir of her journey from immigrant to citizen, appositely entitled *The Promised Land* (1912). In a lesser-known work published only two years later, Antin posed an increasingly important question that continues to divide opinion around the world to this day: do our beliefs in fundamental human rights truly afford anyone a say over restricting new arrivals into a country? As Antin says in *They Who Knock at Our Gates*:

> Let any man who lays claim to any portion of the territory of the United States produce his title deed. Are not most of us squatters here, and squatters of recent date at that? The rights of a squatter are limited to the plot he actually occupies and cultivates. The portion of the United States territory that is covered by squatters' claims is only a fraction, albeit a respectable fraction, of the land we govern. In the name of what moral law do we wield a watchman's club over the vast regions that are still waiting to be staked out? The number of American citizens who can boast of ancestral acres is not sufficient to swing a presidential election.

While nativists across the world spew their hatred, the death toll continues to rise as increasing numbers of people put themselves at risk in order to seek better lives.

After living in exile in Paris and marrying a woman of Vietnamese descent, which was then illegal in his native country, in 1975 the South African painter, poet and activist against apartheid Breyten Breytenbach (1939–) snuck back to South Africa on behalf of Okhela, the anti-apartheid organisation he had helped establish, in order to secure funds for pro-African National Congress activities and establish a network of contacts. Ironically, it was members of the ANC who eventually gave him up to the South African government, which, he later discovered, had been kept abreast of his every step from the outset of his clandestine return. Convicted in late 1975, Breytenbach served two years in solitary confinement in the maximum-security section of Pretoria's prison, incarcerated in a six by five cell. In his ground-breaking collection of essays, *Notes from the Middle World* (2009), part of Breytenbach's 'Middle World Quartet', the South African poet sketches out his definition of what he has called the Middle World, essentially an elusive transnational cultural space that lies beyond one's origins and even one's exile from one's origins. As Breytenbach writes: 'to be of the Middle World is to have broken away from the parochial, to have left 'home' for good (or for worse) whilst carrying all of it with you and to have arrived on foreign shores (at the outset you thought of it as "destination", but not for long) feeling at ease there without ever being "at home".' Is this just exile he asks:

> Maybe. But exile is a memory disease expressing itself in spastic social behaviour: people find it a mysterious ailment and pity you greatly. [...] Exile could be a passage and you may well speak of 'passage people'. Yet, the Middle World is finality beyond exile. For a while at least the reference pole will remain the land from which you had wrenched yourself free or from where you were expelled. Then, exile itself will become the habitat. And in due time, when there's nothing to go back to or you've lost interest, MOR will take shape and you may start inhabiting the in-between. The terrain is rugged, the stage bathed in a dusty grey light. It is not an easy perch.

This serialised essay is excerpted from The Heart of a Stranger: An Anthology of Exile Literature *(Pushkin Press, 2019) which will be published on 8 August.* The Heart of a Stranger *is an anthology of poetry, fiction and non-fiction that journeys through six continents, with over a hundred contributors drawn from twenty-four languages.*

Six Makeshift Trees around My Bathtub

SAMIRA NEGROUCHE

Translated from the French by Marilyn Hacker

Man part animal part flower part metal part human
'The Approximate Man', Tristan Tzara

*

Above our heads   a vertical shadow
                                                vibrates
a shadow that flaps above our heads
a clandestine whistling
on the arid plain   above our overloaded
                                                heads

and while there's that whistling   that whistling
                                    unanticipated
as our buzzing skulls
a cement roof accommodates our moods
            on the makeshift platform
                  the constellation set adrift
in the fog of the senses

you have not abandoned the dusty wreckage
vertical shadows race   at the dunes' edge
your eyes bandaged behind the concave ice
anti-UV protection   not guaranteed

a piano's black keys
                                    at the dunes' edge
a scale that makes no sound

you have not abandoned the dusty wreckage

a vertical shadow
                  planted on the arid plain
that you water with promises
the metallic organ that vibrates
                                    at the edge of a lung
on the cement platform
where the musics clash
protection   not guaranteed
for a makeshift   totem

* *

in the rock garden
a mute man dances
we don't know what funeral oration

they say a deaf man
sows steps of abundance
and solar circles

he was not born to hear
the world exploding

is there a place washed up
on a forgotten ridge
where the news wouldn't arrive
where the news wouldn't be implied
where the news wouldn't be felt
is there a breech in time
that isn't waiting
to fix our gaze
on suffocated screens

are there eyes in this world
ears in this world
that were born
to welcome
into their souls
obscenity
obscenity
obscenity
obscenity
obscenity
and turn away
and not turn away?

* * *

what I like about Jesus
are his faded feet
and those of his companions
– thirteen haloes –
on the abandoned icons
of the small Bulgarian Mount Athos
I'm not talking about the fig tree
– the fig tree Jesus illuminates –
nor of the cascade of rocks
– more like the Grand Canyon than Galilee –
Jesus' delicately faded feet

made me think of the rock paintings
of Tassili
there is no foot as finely
traced as on Hoggar's boulders
they are long slender figures
suspended
exactly like the Christ
suspended fixed and dynamic at once
it's a lightning bolt
an allusion stripped of logic
or so it seems
you find what you find
above all when it's different from what you see
what I like about the astrophysicist
are his premonitions
when he says perhaps
when he says that statistics
have altered physics
fixed it in place
emptied
disembodied
when he says that matter
isn't matter
that time and space
are heresy
that we humans
take ourselves too seriously
thinking ourselves fragile
inventing ourselves powerful
that we invent landmarks
that we forget having invented them
that we must relinquish control
when he says perhaps
give your doubt back its soul

* * * * *

It seems unlikely to me
that a key-word
would open anything whatever
worth the bother
                    words don't open
anything
actually
function paralyses words
I acknowledge   the statistic
paralyses
all the software
by saturation

* * * *

It seems like
a cartoon
tchouri   comet   under surveillance
for the good of humanity   welcome life
matter   organic   welcome
        non-hallucinogenic mushrooms
        preferably
        Japanese
        that seems more serious
        as far as cartoons are concerned
                and micro-*tchouri*
everything is in fact
a game of marbles
marbles of varied size
on a cloth of varied textures
on an infra-silent language
no protection guaranteed
from bubbles
                and scattered micro-lakes
around which chairs are overturned
that can be read as cuneiforms
depending on the branches

network of aquatic bubbles
a solid form
        gaseous
                visible
                        under
my bowl of water seemingly
            isolated
the cradle
of a wireless
network

* * * * * *

a cuneiform language lies
in the branches
of a sacred wood
it holds no secret
that can be translated to sound
it is not the virtual transposition
of any narcissism
barely a dream
a geographical arrangement
of what we call life

there are trees in my head
around my bathtub
because the universe is much too large
far from my puddle of water

Three Poems

JENNIFER EDGECOMBE

Steve Etches's Workbench

half-fossils protective glasses fins pipes hard tissue
not the face I was expecting
memorial bench
Darwin understood the crust of the Earth as a 'history of the world imperfectly kept'
or a 'vast museum'
paternal fascination with babies faces features ears
before clocks
Whitstable Mayday parade 1859
after clocks
the shingle wears the rock away to expose the fossil then the shingle wears that fossil away
a small blue dot   sand
a girl walks to the edge and throws a rock in
plum stones identified from the wreck of the Mary Rose, each unique
like a set of fingerprints
the bell at MEMO* will be rung every time a species becomes extinct
a circular pop noiseless
the sea used to come all the way up to the High Street
he decided to buy the castle and save it
dishes Mrs Ellerbeck had helped her mother bake, who had helped her mother bake who...
archives politics petrol cars
photographs of wavebreaks each one a tidal score
a string of lights at night to remind ourselves we're important
a boy walks to the edge and throws a rock in

---

* Mass Extinction Monitoring Observatory

The Headland of Carbis Bay

is a corner of sedimentary rock
never quite exposed enough
to be walked around.

The sea rushes forward to remove footprints,
forcing walkers
up the emergency rope path.

From this height I have an overwhelming view
of home, refurbished with the orange of this sunset,
the day sliding down my bedroom wall.

I sit with binoculars at low tide searching
for traces of Bessie, Cintra, Vulture, Hampshire,
four wrecks laid down in one night, November 1893.

I see small black dots that could be anything.

The Waverley

You and I were new, drinking on the quay in the extended summer
when the Waverley steamer arrived.
It came in slowly, blocking Sheppey from view.

People looked up from pints and fish.
What is this?
Passengers photographed us and we photographed them.

We cooed and we clicked and we hugged each other.
Watched it dock.
Watched those waiting to get off.

Then, with the sea ahead, it continued its way.
The passengers felt closer this time.
They waved and we waved.

It grew smaller the further out –
that simultaneous feeling of regret and relief
when friends or visitors leave.

Each shingle-stone cast a shadow over the next shingle-stone
in a succession of shadows
and shingle-stones.

We walked home. I saw us –
two figures joined at the hands
with very long legs.

When Allen met Ivan, Peter, Ivan and Laco

Allen Ginsberg's meetings with Slovak Poets

JAMES SUTHERLAND-SMITH

BY 1965, when Ginsberg visited Czechoslovakia, Poland and the Soviet Union, he was *the* avant-garde Anglophone poet who was read in those countries. Barry Miles in his *Ginsberg: a Biography* (2000) cites a conversation with Yevgeny Yevtushenko in 1986 where, in the 1950s, issues of *Evergreen Review* were eagerly passed around and Ginsberg's work was given very careful study. 'You know, in the late fifties, you were my idol,' he told Ginsberg, 'My idol!'

Ginsberg had been translated into Czech and there were royalties waiting for him when he arrived in Prague. However, I wonder how much was lost in translation given the censorship restrictions on subject matter and language. I assume there were officially approved translations of Ginsberg and underground alternatives circulated in *samizdat*.

Ginsberg's visit to Prague between February and May is legendary, but popular summaries give the impression that he had the equivalent of 'a helluva time in Denver' and was too wasted to go anywhere else. Miles provides plenty of juicy detail, but is silent about to whom Ginsberg might have talked about poetry. Jaroslav Seifert, as one of the founders of Poetizmus, which evolved in the 1930s into the Czech version of Surrealism, was in relatively good standing with the Communist Party and Vladimír Holan had his greatest influence on Czech poets in the 1960s. One reason might be that Ginsberg was closely supervised.

The biography does mention his trips to see relatives of his mother in Moscow and his meetings with Yevtushenko and later with Andrei Voznesensky both in Moscow and during Ginsberg's stopover in Warsaw. However, Miles doesn't write anything of his visit to Bratislava in March to meet the three young poets of the Solitary Runners (Osamelí bežci), Ivan Laučík, Peter Repka and Ivan Štrpka, and somebody Ginsberg regarded as Czechoslovakia's equivalent of Pablo Neruda, the poet, Laco Novomeský.

Štrpka mentions Ginsberg's visit in his essay 'Oh, Children Smeared with Honey and with Blood' and how

Ginsberg was a vital influence on the manifesto, 'Return of the Angels' (Návrat anjelov) which asserted against 'the age of ideological interpretation... that the poem should pass the test of a lived experience outside its own language. It would be open and function in unique intimate communication. We said that that the poem is a message of meaning and we quoted Ginsberg to that effect.' In Ján Štrasser's book of conversations with Štrpka, *Living His Poem* (*Žit svoju baseň*, 2018), Štrpka describes Ginsberg's arrival at Bratislava airport where he and Repka had gone to meet him. The book contains a copy of their scribbled note to Laučík to come to Bratislava and a touching photograph of the two young men clutching flowers to greet their hero. However, there was an official reception committee who 'kidnapped' Ginsberg and fobbed off the poets with an instruction to be seen and not heard. He was carried off to the Carlton Hotel, 'the best in town with the best bugs for listening', as Štrpka observed.

The original intention was to have a reading of Ginsberg's poetry, a question and answer session and then the premiere of 'Return of the Angels'. It was clear that the state apparatus was not happy. Miroslav Válek, the poet and later Minister of Culture for Czechoslovakia, warned them: 'Take care they'll want to make Slovak beatniks out of you. Lackeys of Western culture.' It transpired that Ginsberg would perform, but the Solitary Runners not. The theatre was packed. Ginsberg and the Solitary Runners sat on the stage. Actors recited translations of his poems. Ginsberg recited and then talked. Finally a jazz group played. However, the fun was not over. An actor, Fero Vilím, a great supporter of the Solitary Runners, leaped up and announced to the audience, 'There was going to be an introduction of my friends, the young Slovak poets, the Solitary Runners, and now I'm going to read their banned manifesto, "Return of the Angels!".' He proceeded to shout the manifesto at the audience and at the ears of the secret police present, who then, according to Štrpka, 'made life extremely unpleasant for us for many years after'.

Ginsberg wasn't whisked immediately away back to Prague and the Solitary Runners were able to meet him and tour the sites of the old city. In the Jewish cemetery Ginsberg recited his poem, 'At the Grave of Apollinaire', and they drank wine and smoked Mexican weed. Ginsberg left after a lunch with them at the Tatra Hotel and he proposed that they publish their work in English translation with City Lights. For Štrpka and his colleagues it seemed to be a done deal. Yet once Ginsberg was out of the way, 'The Return of the Angels' did not see public light of day for twenty-five years. Ivan Laučík could not publish until the late 1980s and pursued a career as a secondary school teacher in the High Tatras; Ivan Štrpka made a living translating, editing, writing scripts and jazz lyrics; and Peter Repka emigrated to Germany. From the late 1980s onwards, all of them were allowed to publish their accumulated poetry, but only Laučík, who died in 2004, has had a selection of his poems in book form published in English. Štrpka has had a selection in an anthology of six poets, but, despite extensive translation into related Slavic languages, German, Italian, Portuguese and Arabic among other languages, his lack of a book-length selection in English is a serious omission in the Anglophone world's awareness of European poetry.

Ginsberg also met an older poet, Laco Novomeský (1904–76). Novomeský had returned with his family from Prague in the spring of the previous year, having been banned from Slovakia from 1956 and had just been given the honour of being named a National Artist. This followed an official Communist Party rehabilitation in 1963 from his 1954 conviction for treason and sabotage. His readmittance to the Writers' Union was followed by a spate of publications signalled by his first book of poetry for fifteen years, the long poem *Vila Tereza* (1963), and three more books of poetry in close order. By 1965, *Vila Tereza* was in its second edition.

It's necessary to provide a biographical context for the meeting with Ginsberg and Novomeský whose life and career parallels the history of revolutionary Communism, its role in defeating the occupying forces of Nazi Germany, its assumption of political power in post-war Central and Eastern Europe, its domination by Stalinism with attendant purges and the very gradual liberalisation after Stalin's death until the events of 1968 in Czechoslovakia.

Novomeský was born in Budapest and went to school there until 1919 when his family moved to Senica in the south-west of Slovakia. He continued his secondary education and his own poems began to be published while he was still only seventeen. Although he was an external student at Comenius University in Bratislava he soon dropped out to pursue a career in literature and journalism. He had become a committed Communist and by 1924 had met Daniel Okáli (1903–87), Andrej Sirácky (1900–88) and Vladimír Clementis (1902–52), who founded the leading Slovak left-wing literary and political periodical, *DAV*, named after the initials of the Christian names of its founders. An associate of *DAV* was Gustáv Husák (1913–91), later President of Slovakia after 1968. Novomeský's first collection, *Sunday* (*Nedeľa*) appeared in 1927 and in the same year he attended a reception at Vila Tereza, the site of Soviet diplomatic representation to Czechoslovakia. In the 1930s he consolidated his reputation as one of the most important Slovak poets of his generation and became an active advocate of Communism in Czechoslovakia. The title of his second collection, *Romboid*, is commemorated in Slovak culture in the name of one of the leading magazines for contemporary literature. After the Munich agreement Novomeský found it difficult to publish political journalism although he managed a famous article, 'No Farewell to the Slovak and Czech Relationship' ('*Nelúčenie o vzťahu Slovákov a Čechov*').

During the war he continued writing and was active in resistance to the Nazis. It was this activity which provided the pretext for providing Novomeský with near mythical status in a film made shortly after his death, *An Epic About Conscience* (*Poéma o svedomí*, 1978). The film was a popularisation of events during the Slovak national uprising in 1944 against the Nazis. The Communist Party is presented as the sole inspiration and participant in the rising when the truth was otherwise. In the film Husák, Novomeský and Karol Šmidke were the central characters and the irony, considering their post-war fate, could not have been lost on anybody.

Following the war Novomeský became chair of the Slovak Writers' Union and continued writing as a journalist and political activist for the Communist Party. After the takeover of power by the Communist Party in 1948 Novomeský became an important cultural magnate, instrumental in the founding of various Slovak cultural institutions such as a technical university and the Slovak Philharmonic orchestra. He also published his fourth collection of poetry in 1948, *With a Smuggled Pencil* (*Pašovanou cerukou*). In 1946 he suffered the loss of his seven-year old son, Daniel, who had been ill with poliomyelitis.

In 1950 his position changed as he became caught up in the Stalin-initiated purge culminating in the Slanský show trials. He, Husák and Šmidke were gradually stripped of their functions and all three were accused of 'bourgeois nationalism'. In 1951 Novomeský was arrested and interrogated with the purpose of securing a confession for the crimes of treason and sabotage. He and Husák were tried in 1954 (Šmidke had died in 1952 of undisclosed causes after interrogation) and sentenced to ten years' imprisonment. It is said that between 1951 and 1953 Novomeský wrote two epic poems of one hundred six-line verses and two hundred and fifty eight-line verses respectively on cigarette papers which he subsequently used for cigarettes.

Novomeský never served the full ten years. At the end of 1955 he was released under licence and in 1956 his sentence was commuted although he was forbidden to visit Slovakia. He worked at the Literary Institute in Prague from 1957 to 1962 when he began to publish poems again in a Slovak periodical. In 1963 he was rehabilitated and returned to public life being showered with literary honours. He met Ginsberg the following year although it is difficult to know how much Ginsberg knew of Novomeský's personal and political history or indeed of his poetry. The meeting is recalled by Novomeský's daughter, Elena Novomeská-Bútorová with rather different emotions from those of Ivan Štrpka. She wrote to the poet and literary scholar, Ján Gavura in 2012:

> You ask about meeting Allen Ginsberg.
>
> I was there.
>
> My Dad wanted me by his side, quite probably in case something unexpected might occur, of whatever kind, which he, at his age, with illness and previous jail isolation might have not understood or seen because he used to often ask about what was 'normal', regarding for example, technical development.
>
> And this was a situation where I was to be present, because of my English or to serve coffee or just in case he didn't get what was meant. And I was glad because I was very curious about the beatnik.
>
> I think Ginsberg got himself into trouble in Prague, I don't know if he had stripped his clothes off or something like that in his limitless independence and in May in Prague he became King of the May, an annual ritual of students on the 1st May and afterwards he was deported by the police state.
>
> But this happened before.
>
> At the door stood a man, in a long denim coat to the floor, red scarf around his neck long enough also to reach the floor, in white tennis sneakers and something knitted under his coat, hirsute, hair to his shoulders, beard half way down his chest so only his expressively black smart, Picasso-like eyes were to be seen.
>
> Even that was enough.
>
> Luckily, a translator had come along too, a lady who accompanied Ginsberg his whole time in Czechoslovakia. She not only translated exquisitely but also added more to his every question of what the poet meant and wanted to say.
>
> Because all thinking was different and everything was different.
>
> The two worlds met, two opposite peaks.
>
> The beatnik didn't understand how somebody could be locked up when he thought about something differently. The beatnik didn't understand why our poet wouldn't take a chair and go to Hyde Park to explain his ideas. The beatnik, simply, didn't get our system.
>
> My Dad didn't understand how it was that he didn't get it. He'd been here already for a week and had met some writers in Prague. Why hadn't they explained to him that not everything was allowed.
>
> The beatnik behaved freely because he was free, smoked some drugs, told my father that he had a beautiful wife, that was somehow me, and asked when there was going to be a poetry festival. It was simply an utterly different world, freedom. He knew no prohibitions, didn't get, didn't understand the system.
>
> His cleverness was hard to deny but he was here in an era when our young people had never been to the West, never mind to America's West coast. He was a product of his era of hippies, just as we were, especially my Dad, a product of the absolutely different closed, bound, disciplined values that were represented by our police system.
>
> Everything was cheerful, and they said their farewells cheerfully, but the latitude and freedom left and at home remained the pain of an old man and a life weary and hard tested.
>
> This is why he always felt closer to the Russians, to Pasternak, and all this just confirmed that our lives intertwined with pain are more valuable, but also that everything [G]insbergian felt so strange, because he knew nothing of that. Ginsberg wanted to see a poet who had been in prison and went back with an unshakeable belief in socialism, knowing what to think over his whole visit.
>
> *(translated by Ján Gavura)*

Ginsberg went on to his notorious installation as King of the May and his equally notorious dethronement and expulsion from Czechoslovakia. He continued to be curious about and helpful to poets from other countries and politically active until he died in 1997.

Novomeský continued writing poetry and articles, including a celebrated formal poem, 'Requiem' ('Rekviem'). His friendship with Husák, who took over from Dubček as general secretary of the Communist Party after the Soviet invasion of August 1968 and later became president, was compromising. It is claimed that in the spring of 1970 he wrote a personal letter to Husák asking to resign from the Central Committee of the Communist Party because he could not take responsibility for the steps the Party was taking to destroy the 1968 liberalisation of Czechoslovakia. Shortly afterwards he resigned his positions and suffered a severe stroke. He survived a further six years and died in Bratislava.

Philip Emu

MICHAEL FARRELL

Who would hurt Philip?
He was no pillock
That runs down a hillock
And back up a dale
Like a conquering quail
Though he had short legs
He could sit on eggs
He would stalk my hall
And break my balls
Or help with the cryptic
Psychoanalytic
Issues, that arose sometimes
Among the house felines
After too many lives
A shoulder to cry on
Philip emu!
We will all miss you
Those that never met you
Will never forget you
But we will, despite
All the predictably trite
Things we say about dying
And light, the denying
Our refusal to face
The rest of life's race
Without your long neck
Stretched for a peck
Of bread each break-
Fast, you are now the past
Although you look asleep
Soon morticians will creep
Up and take your fleet
Ungainly, grey-black body
Away to the lobby
Of their crematorium
And in memoriam
All we will have is ashes
And as many rashers
(No more beak-fork clashes)
And wheaties as we like
We'll ride our bikes
Without competition

We will have no mission
Of speed without you, Philip
How could they fillet
You right where you stood
You who were so good
So enviably nice
They bashed you twice
On the back of the head
So the coroner said
But who the killer was
Went unmentioned – Ros?
Annie? Benny the Goon?
I hope we know soon
The constant suspicion
Has kept me fishing
For clues and neglecting
My annual reflecting
My biannual vacuuming
Your ghost is looming
Even now Philip, dooming
Me to search each illuminated
Church in the diocese
Affecting criminalese
To try and find out who
Is laying low till you
Are buried and rotten
You were misbegotten
Philip, to come to such
An end I must touch
Wood every hour
Even in the shower
Should I happen to be
There, that, God have mercy
No further poor others
Of favourites or brothers
Will go so violently
So unaccusingly silently
To their undug graves
Still the feathered ghost raves
At night when I try
To get a little shuteye
He won't say goodbye

Till the sun rises red
Then retreats to the shed
With the rest of the depressed
Unavenged and unblessed
Emus and caribous that flew
And sailed, were mailed to zoos
And indulgent peers
Like myself with big ears
And a penchant for deers
And other human-sized
Creatures that disguise
Our dim misanthropy
And terrible photography
And make us tall
And make us fall
In love, and no doubt
Cause jealousy and rout
Of former favourites, where
Is yesterday's hare
For instance, or Philip sparrow
It hurts, like an arrow
To think that I was once
A moaning dunce
Of pain and wonder
Questioning on and under
Bridge for the killers
Of earlier Philips, like Godzilla
Treading my heavy foot
In places it shouldn't be put
Places it wouldn't do good
Places it could only get gout
Thinking north, or south?
Whoever performed the fatal hit
I blame the whole north for it
Philip never really belonged
I never heard his song
Which was said to be sweet
And had its own beat
As well. Philip – get to hell
You'll at least be warmer
Than you were this summer
In this world, with this worm

An I who is a he

Monk's Eye, Cees Nooteboom, translated from the Dutch by David Colmer (Seagull) £12.99

Reviewed by ANTHONY BARNETT

It is, I believe, fairly common for a great poet to produce a prose work – fiction, essay, autobiography – that is at least interesting, and sometimes much more than that. It is not often that a great novelist writes interesting poetry. Cees Nooteboom, author of, for example, such marvelous stories as *The Following Story* and *A Song of Truth and Semblance*, also an essayist, is one exception. Poetry is, in fact, central to his life. Previously translated by David Colmer for Seagull are Nooteboom's selected poems *Light Everywhere* and, with artist Max Neumann, the truly remarkable *Self-Portrait of an Other*, which might inadequately be described as a unified sequence of prosepoems. I know that Colmer is a trustworthy translator. I first read *Self-Portrait* in an earlier translation in a review. I had the original and I thought that the translation was good and true. Then I read Colmer's and understood how much more work he had done.

Monk's Eye is a poem in thirty-three parts. I would have said poems but Nooteboom's postscript describes the whole in the singular. Each part, then, is made up of three irregular, unrhymed quatrains, plus one more line which he has described elsewhere as a cauda, rather than a coda. The thirty-third part has a further cauda: 'The murmur of the sea', repeated three times. *Monk's Eye* was written on two islands, the Frisean Schiermonnikoog ['Grey Monk Eye' – *schier* is an old word for *grey*], settled by the Cistercians, and Minorca, where Nooteboom spends his summers, so the sea and the shore, and 'Phaedrus and Socrates on the path through the dunes', are indeed everywhere. I happen to know that not all of the poem refers to its author, but to another, as in: 'In the end the old poet wanted nothing more / to do with the sea. Something so wide and open / terrified him, he said, he saw his / transparent life in a transparent // death.' Yet, *Monk's Eye* is also like a selfportrait, in common with the earlier *Self-Portrait*: 'An I who is a he, a him who is me, images of an island that becomes another island (an archetypal *insular*), and then itself again', opens the postscript.

I think the poem is a non-confessional confession (Nooteboom was schooled by monks). It recounts memories of childhood and adulthood modified in non-chronological (well, the thoughts are chronological but not the events) dreamlike trances interspersed with discussion of what it means for the author to write, to write poetry: 'Try it, only words left, no feelings, the power / of them being themselves, you no longer existing', but what does this mean: 'Never give a poem a difference. / That ends in disaster.'? I wouldn't like to say but it is part of the response to 'The marten asked, What is evening?', as is: 'The monk curled up, / a flake of holiness, I know / what I know, said the evening / and disappeared into the cliff face // with no goodbye'.

I'd like to say a word about the production. Italian, Spanish, German versions, the latter illustrated by Matthias Weischer, one-time disciple of David Hockney, are bilingual. Our English version is not. Nooteboom's original is illustrated only with a cover photo of the sea by Simone Sassen. *Monk's Eye* includes nine intricate colour 'digital collages' by Sunandini Banerjee. They are pretty, visibly inspired, in Indian manner, by the poem, but they are, to my mind, a publisher's indulgence. Admittedly, they may make a book of poetry appear more attractive to some readers. They are intermittent throughout the book, on left-hand pages. The poem parts are on right-hand pages. This means that the seventy-two-page cloth book has, irregularly, quite a few blank pages. I would not bother with the following trifle but for the fact that the Seagull School of Publishing offers courses 'run entirely by industry professionals'. Why, then, is *Monk's Eye* set in a typeface where the kerning is wrong when a word ends with the letter 'f' (too much space)? This is a fairly widespread fault with digital type. But one does not have to live with it. There are faces without this fault. Where there is this fault it can be rectified without difficulty, as I learnt to my benefit when I contacted Monotype about a favorite typeface. Yet, one is only grateful to Seagull for seeking out Nooteboom for his poetry.

'Think up a past, do not skimp / on war or infidelity.' And 'Why don't the dead leave us in peace? / They scatter their names over the road / we have to walk, insert their lines of verse / in our last bit of sleep before morning, // then go again, absent as if / it's a profession [...] memories / without appointments.'

Like a Sausage

Jane Yeh, *Discipline* (Carcanet) £9.99

Reviewed by MAITREYABANDHU

Jane Yeh's poems are at their best when estranged, deadpan comedy touches a sore spot: loneliness, failed romance, fear. In *Discipline*, her third and arguable best collection, this tension between droll comedy and private suffering is at its most disquieting. Reading Jane Yeh is like listening to an eccentric aunt tell absurd stories while she rings for the maid to clear away the breakfast things: we can hear the tinkle of the far-off bell in a freezing scullery or some filthy back kitchen, but the room we're sitting in is perfectly delightful. The effect is one of intense privacy despite all the charm.

In part, Yeh achieves this effect by seeming to describe ordinary things in an ordinary way, without embellishments or poetics. But this is subterfuge: what we actually get is peculiar things, oddly described. There is something twisted at work. The self-consciously flat style, the list-like end-stopped or almost end-stopped lines, the drollery, the eschewal of elaborate syntax are all of a piece with her bad-girl urbanity and lack of sentimentality. Ironic and askance, these poems *cannot be serious*, and yet one has a horrible feeling that they are. It is like watching Buster Keaton as another falling building narrowly misses him.

And the falling buildings in *Discipline* are indeed funny. In the wonderful 'Self Portrait as a Spinster', for instance, we hear that, 'To be unloved is like listening to a progress report on courgettes – for months'. This comes in one flat, can't-be-bothered-with-enjambment line. Later in the same poem we read, 'It was okay to be alone, like a sausage in a garden full of flowers' – picking up, perhaps, on its faint reference to Wordsworth's 'lonely as a cloud' and those daffodils. Comedy in *Discipline* is not always evasive, sometimes it's just a good gag: 'Pizza will come in two sizes: snack and preposteroso' ('Utopia Villas') and, 'If this movie could talk, it would have a squeaky voice like a nerd in a Hollywood movie, even though most nerds actually have normal voices' ('These Movies'). But at its sharpest, the laughs of *Discipline* are hollow, black, tragicomic laughs, tinged with desperation: 'Behind every day is another // Freaking day: run and gun, trail of breadcrumbs, / The bureau of shrunken heads' ('The Detective'). Even Yeh's use of old-fashioned initial caps, forming a spine down the poem, enhances the conscious stiffness and alienation of her voice; they help make the poems squeak and shriek: 'Some of the Cats, / Played drastic minuets on diminutive grand pianos.' ('A Short History of Destruction'):

> The traffic stops and goes past, a mechanical river.
> A siren goes off in the distance somewhere, like somebody crying.
> ('Happy Hour, New York City')

The pain here is not merely private, however. There is nothing self-absorbed about Yeh's work. Reading her three Carcanet collections, one learns next to nothing about her. At best we glean a likening for cats and women's fashion; an interest in art (John Singer Sargent in *The Ninjas*, Watteau in *Marabou*, 1970s performance art and Kirsten Glass in *Discipline*); a taste for mixing high and low subject matter; and a sense of humour. In this new collection, the persistent background loneliness of *The Ninjas*, with its robots and androids, its 'Attack of the Crystalline Entity', opens out to include larger themes: climate change, migration and violence. In the perfectly judged 'A Short History of Migration', for instance, pain is communal and historical. Yeh is the daughter of Taiwanese migrants, so the subject has personal significance too. But she will not indulge. The deadpan humour is used to devastating effect: 'We ate the same meal seventeen days in a row (pancakes).' Then later, 'We hindered our children with violins, bad haircuts, and diplomas.'

There is so much to enjoy in *Discipline,* such as 'The Detectives', 'Self-Portrait as New York in the Eighties' and the strange love poem 'A Short History of Patience': '*Won't you come home?* / Says the dustpan to the wandering broom'. 'True Facts About the Herring Gull' – 'Most of the cries mean *Give me your chips*' – along with the very oblique self-portrait 'The Rhinos' and the tender 'Pacific Pocket Mouse', which add to her growing list of admirable animal poems. But there are dangers. Firstly, the danger of whimsy, of the poems ending up as mere oddities: weightless, for a single reading only. Secondly, the very flatness of the style can become rather too self-consciously stylish – a fashionable 'estrangement' sliding into a merely alienated account of how alienated we are:

> Every line
> Is a performance that won't stay up. My kingdom for a joke.
> ('Self Portrait as Klaus Nomi in New York')

Thirdly and lastly there is the danger of a kind of chic, risk-free nihilism, where everything is meaningless and therefore a bit of a joke (imagine the New Testament recited by Andy Warhol). Yeh seems aware of this danger, closing 'Poem in Which All the Questions Are Answered' with, 'When it's over, you can pretend you never cared about it anyway'. But it is a temptation. If I were a member of some kind of intergalactic poetry police force sent to earth to admonish versifiers, I'd scribble 'Excellent!' in the margins of most of the poems in *Discipline*, then I'd caution her to write a book-length poem about growing up in New Jersey with Taiwanese parents.

Ariadne

Ruth Padel, *Emerald* (Chatto) £10

Reviewed by ALASTAIR LLEWELLYN-SMITH

Ruth Padel's eleventh collection, *Emerald*, was conceived, she has written, as an exploration of the role this gemstone has played in history, mining and myth, as magical talisman or tradable commodity; and of green, in its many different shades and associations, including the colour of nature. But the project changed direction, she has explained, when her mother fell ill, and died three weeks after being rushed to hospital. *Emerald* then became all about leave-taking, dying and her mother's life. The poems are tender, acutely observed and sometimes funny:

tell me how many men
did your mother
sleep with   really? I've always wondered.
  ('Intermission')

Each of the thirty poems is self-contained, but, like Ariadne, Padel has given the reader a ball of thread that links the first to the last page. The very first line is 'This is to do with being lost' and the last poem, 'Salon Noir', which is an exploration of (and meditation on) the eponymous painted chamber in the pre-historic caves of Niaux in the Ariège, ends:

  But the mountains
rising one behind the other
  were herds of green bison
drifting away into the sky.

The bison have escaped from their cavernous walls, now reborn as mountains grazing the sky. Padel is very good at echoing an image or a thought many pages after the first sounding, so that the reader has to backtrack to recover the allusion. Similarly, rhymes are carried from one poem to others later on, e.g. 'crust' on page 7 ('Astray') reappears on page 40 ('Carbon Labyrinth') and is echoed as 'rust' on page 48 ('Postern').

There is an arresting originality to her starting points:

I captured the first tear
rolling down my cheek
with a micro-pipette.
  ('The Crystallization of Tears')

The new collection contrasts strongly with some of her earlier books, such as *Learning to Make an Oud in Nazareth*, and its narrative poems, e.g. 'A Guide to the Church of Nativity in Time of Siege', which evokes Browning's 'Fra Lippo Lippi'. In *Emerald*, Padel illustrates the distance between life and death – the gap between love lived and love remembered – in the structure of the poems:

The little daily shock
that she is not
still   flicking her fins
in the solitary kitchen.
  ('Logbook')

That 'not' pulls the reader up short, highlighting the poignancy of 'solitary kitchen'.

There isn't a single comma in any of the poems (apart from two in one of the titles). In its place, Padel uses gaps of a constant width between words, as a pause for breath, a sparking into life of the reader's imagination. 'Tuning Your Lyre Among the Shades' describes being winched down into an emerald mine:

  I don't belong
here nothing human possibly could.

Could a comma or a dash instead of that gap between 'here' and 'nothing' provide the same jolt? And again:

wavelengths of memory   tangled as the ancient cottons
in her long abandoned sewing-casket
  ('Part-Arc of a Rainbow')

'Casket' in place of 'basket' is especially effective. So, too, is her echo (in 'The Crystallization of Tears') of the great Jewish affirmation, *L'Chaim* – to Life, with its five keening 'aye' rhymes:

Here's to goodbye. Here's to the tears
I knew I'd cry. She'd have loved
how each fresh-minted sphere

crystallizes as it dries
in its own one-off design. Tomorrow
I'm going to x-ray every drop and find out why.

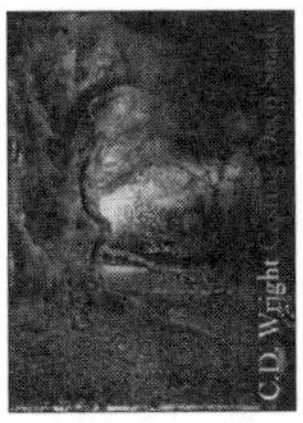

After Narrative

C.D. Wright, *Casting Deep Shade* (Copper Canyon Press) $32

Reviewed by VALERIE DUFF

Casting Deep Shade, a second posthumous publication by C.D. Wright, is a one-hundred-and-sixty-page intensive study of the beech tree. One wonders if, had Wright lived, the book might have been reshaped into something more aligned with the verse of her early collaborative project with photographer Deborah Luster, *One Big Self*, about the world of those incarcerated in Louisiana's state prisons. As it is, *Casting Deep Shade* is more encyclopedic than verse, a book of lore the experimental Wright makes feel effortless. While more prose than poetry, it is poetic in temperament, temperature. True to the quirky and unmistakable voice of Wright's oeuvre, *Casting Deep Shade* is a commonplace book of nature for a world entering an artificial age.

In *Casting Deep Shade* – with its monomaniacal reflections on, of all things, the beech – the tree is all (Joyce Kilmer's poem springs to mind, and does, in fact, make an appearance). This book about the beech tree has all the considered haphazardness, the leaping history, of Anne Carson's *Nox*, as Wright forms narratives that range disjointedly from family snapshot to human history, from esoteric information to sharp lyric. Wright focuses on the moments when beech intersects with the human, as in this vignette about painter David Hockney (which ends in a woodpile):

> In the spring of 2009 when David Hockney returned to a familiar copse to paint the beeches and sycamores near his home, he found 'a massacre'. Planted a hundred years ago as a shelter for farm building and fields, they had been felled as they presented a safety issue for the nearby cottages. Planted as a windbreak. Downed as a hazard. The property now owned by a kitchen tycoon. Chop chop.
>
> (Two Hockneys, summer & winter, had been completed before the massacre.)
>
> Nobody asked about those trees. Nobody asks enough questions anymore.
> The painter rued.
>
> I think now, says Hockney, this is my next painting of the wood. It will be very
> different, but the piles of wood are quite beautiful in their own right, simply because:
>
> wood
> can't help
> being
> beautiful.

Whether she focuses on the beeches of Birnham wood, or tells of the study of trees at Los Alamos, 'town without pity', Wright's authority is firm, backed by copious notes at the end. Even before one examines the documented research, one feels the weight of her project (*ShallCross*, also published after her death in 2016, while more representative of her verse, doesn't have the same heft and ambition). The language is as meticulous, as exacting as that in her acclaimed book-length poem *Deepstep Come Shining*. As always, Wright hones the story to its meaning:

> Thomas Jefferson ordered purple beeches from Thomas Main's nursery in 1807.
> Planted them at Monticello. The first spring planting failed; so he ordered them
> again in the fall. One blew down in the 1950s (its replacement fell to disease in
> 2001), the other lived until the 1970s.
>
> The trees must have been planted by Wormley Hughes-grandson of Elizabeth Heming, born at Monticello – a slave, who started working there as a boy. Though he was freed by Martha Randolph, his wife and eight children were sold to a University of Virginia prof. Most were brought back together later on the plantation of Thomas Randolph, Jefferson's grandson. Among the many holes Mr. Hughes dug, one was the President's grave.

By unearthing the strange, destructive, worshipful stories that exist around these trees, she captures avatar and holy relic in a book both studied and imaginatively free. She blows in bits of her own life, then moves to Yeats and 'the copper beech near Gort which Lady Gregory encouraged her guests to autograph' and then considers the marring of the beech with graffiti. Is this a book of poems? Wright falls into verse when narrative won't suffice:

> So Tennyson sat on a 'serpent-rooted beech.'
>
> X meant HONEY HERE. It still means honey here.
>
> Honey, *if* the bees be with us.
>
> (If we go, *says the cartoon bee's speech bubble*, we're taking you with us.)
>
> As one scientist put it, *We* are the asteroid.

Darker and less pithy than the bee in Dickinson's 'To make a prairie', the writing leaves the late Wright's voice intact; she is a poet of the Ozarks facing the blindness of the modern age.

Wright is often described as iconoclastic, idiosyncratic. Perhaps this is because she is a female poet, lived to a certain age, who broke with conconventional form and ideas of poetry and held her own. But beyond her staying power, her prolificness, her rich and identifiable voice, there is something else, captured in this last book particularly – her ability to both retain and let go of herself in the story. This is her great achievement, whether one loves the beech tree or not – to enter into C.D. Wright's love for it, love for the earth, for nature, and for imperfect beings, capable of creating and destroying, who walk within it. She ends prophetically, sympathetically, with lines from W.S. Merwin: 'On the last day of the world / I would want to plant a tree.'

'more or less everything'

Chris Wallace-Crabbe, *Rondo* (Carcanet) £9.99

Reviewed by WILLIAM POULOS

In *Rondo* (a word which derives from an Old French term meaning 'round'), Wallace-Crabbe revisits themes which occupied his earlier poems. This is not, however, meant to discount the pleasant variety of this collection and his poetry; there are still a hundred things to see before we get back home. Forms and themes adjoin to create a landscape like the diverse Aussie ones Wallace-Crabbe describes: the poems which don't rhyme and scan sit with poems in quatrains and couplets. There is even a villanelle which undercuts the traditional pastoral theme by evoking hayfever, and this mix of the formal and informal characterises Wallace-Crabbe's work.

What he does best is make you re-examine the things you've seen many times before; in the poem 'Bits and Pieces' he affirmed the importance of comfortable underwear (often taken for granted) and *Rondo* includes a poem about a sharpener, which begins:

> Soft cedar turns against this blade
> Coming away in aromatic flakes.
> The red of a Staedtler stains an edge
> Of these rising, falling petals [...]

Here Wallace-Crabbe hasn't just adorned the pencil with the characteristics of a flower; the polysyllabic and sensuous word 'aromatic' gives it gravity and beauty, and the slow fourth line ensures the reader doesn't pass by it too quickly. Wallace-Crabbe shows us that the everyday is important, which is why his poetry is full of demotic diction: 'she's got the game by the balls', 'Fair enough', 'Get real'.

His colloquialism facilitates even his poems on harrowing subjects: 'Rendition', starkly describing the fear of torture ('not something pushed right up under your fingernails / nor a bloody gobbet hacked off your left ear'), is one of his most affecting poems. Yet in other poems the solemn subject matter produces pleonasms and stiffness: in 'Fragrant Here All Day', a poem which includes the colloquial phrases 'the fatness of my purse', and 'willy-nilly', the narrator responds to some gangs' ambitions for power by saying that 'such is the opposite of all we want'. 'Maybe, Now', a vague rebuke against free-market economics, predicts a financial crash sometime in the future, or, more precisely, 'when the fan has been thoroughly shitted'. Reading this line, I imagine a malfunctioning robot shooting spare parts out of its rear end. 'And The Cross' presents the reader with more clumsiness: the poem's rhyming quatrains retell the story of Jesus and say that Joseph and Mary spent the night in a stable because they didn't have the 'financial pull' to stay anywhere nicer. Maybe they could have afforded it if they'd had 'money', but then that wouldn't rhyme. Wallace-Crabbe exploits the form well. The poem ends:

> His legacy? Make your own minds up.
> Did Roman nails deserve his blood?
> Even for someone who venerates money
> Here is a story of absolute good.

In fact, the poem does nothing to convince you that the story of Jesus is an absolute good, and this flat final line with the half-rhyme of 'blood / good' contributes to a sense of disappointment. Agnosticism has featured in Wallace-Crabbe's earlier poems, and indeed in the first stanza of this poem he admits that he doesn't know what to make of Jesus's story. Instead, he puts his faith in words: *Rondo* is full of references to other writers and to language itself. Words are 'more or less everything' and even bestow an afterlife: 'Rendition' reminds you that you will die, but also that 'you will survive, language holding some trace of you for years'.

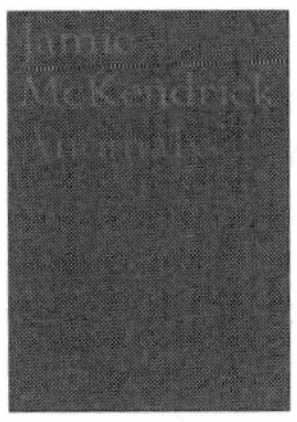

Practice and Theory

Jamie McKendrick, *Anomaly* (Faber) £14.99; Philip Hancock, *City Works Dept* (CB Editions) £8.99

Reviewed by ROBERT SELBY

'I keep forgetting if this is / Lucerne or Geneva, Geneva or Lucerne', writes Jamie McKendrick in his characteristically well-travelled new collection, *Anomaly*. This, seventh, gathering of poetical dispatches from across Europe reminds us that his erudition is a borderless, cosmopolitan one, lightly borne if sometimes erring into caricature: 'I was eating alone in Arezzo, / eavesdropping on the conversation of Yves / Bonnefoy who happened to be at the next table'. This is a Renaissance man whose learnedness has opened doors beyond the world of 'petty, internecine poetry': subversion is gate-crashing the British Council's party at the 'glut of money and art' that is the Venice Biennale. Inside, he reflects that the Venetian artist Canaletto lost his inspiration after living for a time in London; if he were there now, 'he'd be a bargaining chip'. McKendrick conforms to the English intelligentsia's traditional embarrassment with home, Brexit only confirming a belief in its benightedness. For him, England's tastelessness is encapsulated by Liverpool's fake Gothic, 'marzipannish pink' St Michael-in-the-Hamlet church which is 'still, / worse luck, more home to me / than any mosque or duomo / in peerless travertine or marble'.

England is embodied, too, by his father, reduced to a shrunken realm of palliative care, reliving the war, the so-called national sense of 'fair play' one of the last things to fade. Father informs son of the German colonel near Bremen he patched up as best he could:

> In the night he shouts for my sister,
> demands she call an ambulance
> this minute, can't she see
> the colonel's dying, he points to the floor,

it's a bloody disgrace
to leave him lying there.

Age and the only end of age are recurring preoccupations in this collection, perhaps not coincidentally the first to be published in McKendrick's seventh decade – a potential hinge point between 'a jaundiced mortal pallor / and golden life,' as he perceptively describes the colour of the quince in a Juan Sànchez Cotàn painting. He finds affinity with the horses in 'The Urban Field' that 'philosophically survey / the mode of transport that replaced them', and begins 'feeling my age – / breathless, bereft, my only field the page'. But two of the collection's finest poems offer hope, however misplaced, of death's indefinite forestalment: in 'Reprieve', the fact that broken bones can mend suggests 'time's arrow doesn't always have to rush / thoughtlessly forward but can choose to stop / mid-air'; 'To a Dried-up Elm', meanwhile, lends the eponymous old tree by the Duero continued life by recording it:

Turned to the light, to the life it might bring,
  my heart as much as yours awaits
  another miracle of spring.

Intimations of mortality, and his having had a *Selected Poems* published in 2016 that surveyed twenty-five years of work, have McKendrick regrouped and combative, standing up for his *oeuvre* against 'some spotty fledgling in the *Avian Times*' who 'calls my song "awkward" and "uninspired"' and tilting at one critic who wished him 'some adversity in his future, as on the evidence of his work little seems to have ruffled his affluent composure'. Steeped as it is in literary and ekphrastic allusions, translations – beautiful ones – from the Italian of Valerio Magrelli, and with some of Western Europe's most refined quarters for its backdrops, McKendrick's poetry will attract misplaced accusations of elitism. But the most lethal charge is its being 'uninspired', and the *Selected Poems* did betray a progressive loss of pressure from his 1991 debut *The Sirocco Room* and 1993's *The Kiosk on the Brink* – taut missives from the *bel paese* that struck this grey isle as vividly exotic as the contemporaneous ones by James Richardson on Channel 4's *Football Italia* – to 2012's saggy *Out There*. In its energy, however, *Anomaly* is suggestive of a second spring, and it is a testament to the self-deprecation of the man himself that, ending one poem calling out a critic, McKendrick acknowledges that a friend's ostensibly encouraging words – 'When the dogs bark, that means you're really moving' – were delivered by Sancho Panza to Don Quixote when the Don was 'galloping away at what he took to be breakneck speed, mounted on the clapboard flanks of a rocking horse'.

McKendrick, born in Liverpool in 1955, has lived his adult life across a continent of intellectual exchange. Philip Hancock, born in 1966, lived the formative years of his in Stoke-on-Trent, leaving school at sixteen to serve a City & Guilds craft apprenticeship and work alongside decorators, glazers and joiners for whom reading, let alone writing poetry, might seem to be – to quote another poet from a working-class background, Douglas Dunn – 'the sort of thing a Jessie would do'. In the poem 'Knowing One's Place' from *City Works Dept*, his debut, Hancock hides a copy of Albert Camus's *L'Étranger* inside 'Stoke City's / '79 season first team pull-out' to serve as alibi should his workmates enquire into his lunchbreak reading. 'After the miles behind, / the years catching up', Hancock laments, the only time a flicker of regret comes over a collection quietly proud of the skill of, and camaraderie between, the many characterful tradesmen it describes, a pride that never slips into the saccharine.

The collection's world is a fading one of community cohesion, of Clarks shoe shop and the mobile library (with its 'County lettering / in gold leaf'), valued apprenticeships and trades, employment provided by the 'pot banks' – pottery factories – and their supply chains, and Ritzy's nightclub on a Friday or Saturday to let the hair down. The poem 'Apprentice', in which Hancock, while whitewashing skylights, surveys market day in Tunstall carrying on below him, recalls 'all the morning of the town' in Dylan Thomas's *Under Milk Wood* or the poems in Dunn's *Terry Street* about the titular working-class street in Hull. Here, though, we're on first-name terms; these are people and not the romanticised 'gods' of Dunn's 'pantheon of boots and overalls':

        Gorgeous
Trish swallow-dives across her fruit and veg
and Darlo flicks a fag end from the Sneyd Arms steps.

I stand among lions, gargoyles and angels,
watch my good friend John, apprenticed
to the undertaker, waxing the Daimler.

The lions, gargoyles and angels are, of course, heraldic mirrors of the citizens themselves: the old seamen turned decorators keeping in shape with badminton on Thursdays; the cricket-playing tradesman who beds other men's wives in the back of his minivan; 'The Quiet Joiner' hanging fifteen sapele fire doors in three days without a word; neighbour Kerry Davies with her 'paprika Afro', who grows up to play football for England; the scaffolders sometimes viewed by other trades as being on the bottom rung but who have 'heights and levels sussed at a glance, / no hands at forty feet in the rain, / working for each other' and, in the caff after, swaggering on their danger money. This last example is indicative of Hancock's first-hand appreciation for the tradesman's taken-for-granted specialist skill and knowledge, often as dexterous as any art. Memorably, in the poem 'Top Storey', Hancock, reaching the end of his ladder, glimpses a 'flash of arse, slammed door / as I appear', but his only desire is windows:

windows that slide sweetly, overlap
enough for painting the middle rail,
for the gloss to flow just right
and cut in sharp to the edge,
everything reachable, no snags,
not her coming back from the shower.

The thematic results of McKendrick's appreciation of the cerebral and Hancock's of the practical are thus not dissimilar, and as poets they have in common a gift for acutely observed, compressed portraits in which every word does heavy lifting. Theirs are different worlds of equal importance, England the richer for having both McKendrick's restaurant *cicoria e fagioli* and Hancock's 'tea, orange squash, biscuits on paper plates'.

'Something We Have in Common'

We Begin in Gladness, Craig Morgan Teicher (Graywolf) $16

reviewed by JONATHAN FARMER

I almost stopped reading Craig Morgan Teicher's *We Begin in Gladness* before I'd even finished the introduction.

To be fair, it wasn't anything specific to his book that I objected to. Rather, it was something I've been seeing a lot of lately – and seeing with increasing exasperation each time. This example comes from Teicher's book,[1] but you could find something similar in a lot of recent writing on poetry:

> implicitly, poems probe the unknown, beginning on firmer ground and speaking until they have expressed the otherwise inexpressible, something sayable only in those words, in that poem. Poets work to express the questions roiling beneath their statements, the statements beneath their questions. Poets rarely trust assertions.

It's tricky business, defining poetry. Any circle that tries to sum Lucretius, Longfellow, Petrarch, Lorca, Lucile Clifton, Robert Lowell, conceptual poetry, limericks, poems of political protest and the civil service exams of the Tang dynasty will either include a lot of things that obviously aren't poetry, exclude a lot of things that obviously are, or just cease being a circle altogether. (At least as far back as Aristotle people have been trying to define it as something distinct from its recognisable forms of composition, with consistently odd results.)

There was a time in the history of English poetry (and in the shorter history of the word's existence in English) when it would have been possible to say what poetry was – language organised sonically into some kind of regular and recognisable pattern. (It's because of those patterns, and their legacy, that most poems leave so much white space on the page, not, as Teicher claims, because 'A certain amount of loneliness – an awareness of the unsayable – is a precondition for poetry.') These days, the best definition of poetry I can imagine is almost pointlessly imprecise: writing that intends to participate in one of the countless traditions and trajectories that originate in the writing composed under those earlier conditions. And there's a lot in those traditions that just doesn't accord with the idea that poetry does or should express 'the otherwise inexpressible, something sayable only in those words, in that poem', including much of the earliest poetry, whose function was often communal, dogmatic, and even practical. As recently as the eighteenth century, Alexander Pope praised wit – for him, the true end of poetry – as 'Nature to advantage dress'd, / What oft was thought, but ne'er so well express'd'. And people haven't stopped writing poems that live outside of Teicher's definition in the centuries since.

If it were just one person writing this, or if it he'd written it in a slightly different way, I imagine I could have kept my pedantic tendencies in check and just moved on. After all, he's giving a pretty accurate assessment of longstanding and productive fashions in American poetry and criticism. What really bothered me, I suspect, was that in so many cases he was describing not just poetry – which is made up of poems, which we can all read and debate and describe for ourselves – but poets.

A little later, Teicher writes of *his* beginnings as a poet around the age of fourteen. It's a lovely description, starting with the death of his mother, of whom he writes, 'I used to tell her everything, talk to her constantly every day of my life':

> Poetry was, it is now obvious to me, my response to the shock of suddenly having no one to address everything to. I had nothing in particular to say, but needed to say something, to anyone, to everyone.
>
> So, poetry was a natural fit. And when I began to learn, in my tenth-grade honors English class, of the many people who had devoted their lives to it throughout history, I was hooked. It's a sad origin story, I know, but it has compensated me with a life filled with joy and interest, with a community of brilliant and obsessed people, toward objects for my devotion.

I think that's why I get so upset: Teicher and others seem to be defining who belongs in that community, and these definitions seem unnecessarily small, which diminishes not only what gets said, and how, but who gets invited to speak.

*

I did keep reading – and I'm glad I did.

Teicher writes, in his chapter on W.S. Merwin: 'The staggering thing about a life's work is that it takes a lifetime to complete. Which is to say having a writer's collected writings means having a chance to comprehend a life, or a life's summary, in terms of whatever part of a self makes art [...] How remarkable, to be able to imagine a person's whole gaze.'

More often than not, *We Begin in Gladness* tells the story of a life as lived in writing remarkably well, especially when he spends an entire chapter on a poet, which allows him room to move the poems around in different lights. Among the shorter treatments, the standout is an imaginative, attentive four-page description of Delmore Schwartz's 'The Heavy Bear Who Goes With Me', which ends:

> What can a poem accomplish simply by being read, by being tolerated, even enjoyed until the end? Why do any of us confess to the wrong we've done? What do we want in return? Forgiveness, of course, as I said. But what's so remarkable about Schwartz's poem is the way it gets what it needs: by reading it, enjoying it, singing and savoring its music, don't we forgive it? Aren't we implicitly admitting that this bear, this Delmore Schwartz, has powerful charms? All we have to do is get to the bottom of the page, and Schwartz is forgiven his whole miserable life.

---

1 In the interest of transparency: I've met Teicher twice and published his writing several times as well. While we don't know each other well, he has been consistently generous and kind in our limited interactions.

From the Archive

Issue 147, September–October 2002

JEREMY OVER

From a contribution of three poems including 'Your Awful Voice' and 'Tring'. Fellow contributors to this issue include Carola Luther, Sinéad Morrisey, Marilyn Hacker, R.F. Langley, Geoffrey Hill, Robert Minhinnick and John Ashbery.

NOT BUT NOW AND THEN

I might perhaps dip and wash a little
and collecting all in skimming close
the land begins to think in woods tempered with salt
as summer declines all day long in the wet borders.

How strange is it in my field though
meeting a shoe, the face of the sky
darkening, drowned at an angle
and never seen till seldom squeals
the lakes and mill ponds building a rather rather
marooned in the steeples?

It is up to you Mr Crabtree.
I'd rather not raise their wings
and make them loquacious
late as Michaelmas, I am etc.
most shy and wild fine grasses.

Teicher is a smart and companionable critic, frequently relaxed, consistently perceptive, available, as in the passage above, to his own passions, as well as others'. Among those things that remain true of almost all poems is that they're written by and for people, and Teicher's particular human presence in the book allows him to render the ways in which one person might value a given poem while also writing imaginatively about the person who wrote it. He once again records the potential complexity of that encounter when he writes of Sylvia Plath's 'Daddy', with its borrowed suffering:

> As a Jew whose grandparents came to America fleeing Hitler's takeover of Austria, I have a hard time not taking this personally, but that's precisely what's always drawn me to it [...] She's gone too far, but I can't help but admire the success of her communication: she's leapt out of her head, crossed time, cheated death, and pissed me off more than fifty years later.

Though I've never found 'Daddy' as compelling as Teicher does, I'm intrigued by what he makes of it, in particular by the humility with which he describes the meaning of his own emotional response. The passage – like many of the poems I love – surprises me as an image of one way a person can be in the encounter, attempted or actual, with another.

Teicher's depiction of Plath's movement from apprentice to extraordinary is in some ways akin to his description of his own beginnings: 'I had nothing in particular to say, but needed to say something, to anyone, to everyone.' The leap came only after she could, he writes, 'find subjects suitable to her voice and craft, subjects that would push and then exceed the frames of her technique'. His description of 'The Colossus' rings true:

> The poem's subject is no longer what's being looked at but the looking itself, or, more precisely, the strained psyche behind the eyes that distorts what's being seen. Plath's extraordinary verbal inventiveness has begun to find a subject equal to it: the limitless shapeshifting the mind exerts on the world, the ways the heart can inflect, even infect, what happens.

Two chapters in the book are especially good: the one on W.S. Merwin and the one (a half-chapter, really) on John Ashbery. In looking across the careers of both poets, Teicher sifts confidently between the poems that seem best and those periods and tendencies that fall short. He does so without vanity of self-display, and in ways that consistently clarify the larger body of work.

Teicher describes Ashbery as both "a collage artist and a metaphysical philosopher," and though he articulates the early virtues of the collage artist with imagination, it's the metaphysician who interests him most, especially the one that materialises in 'Self-Portrait in a Convex Mirror'. 'Elsewhere in his poetry,' Techer explains, 'instability merely functions to prove its own insistence, but here it illustrates something we have in common.'

After 'Self-Portrait', as Teicher notes, Ashbery seemed to mechanise his brilliance. 'He has a point – many points – to make,' Teicher writes, 'while vocabulary changes over time, its utility and its limitations stay about the same. But.' He continues, 'if that *is* the point, it flies in the face of what many of us hope poetry can accomplish: the construction of a bridge – albeit a flimsy one – between inner and outer worlds.'

Criticism can also serve as such a bridge, naming the experience a particular work of art might conjure imaginatively enough that the name itself, addressed to that same work of art – or another that resembles it – can conjure that experience too. In spite of my frustrations at the outset, *We Begin in Gladness* frequently does that unusually well.

Ordinary Wonder

Helen Dunmore, *Counting Backwards: Poems 1975–2017* (Bloodaxe Books) £14.99

Reviewed by EDMUND PRESTWICH

Counting Backwards: Poems 1975–2017 is a generous selection of Helen Dunmore's poetry, adding three subsequent collections and some earlier poems to *Out of the Blue: Poems 1975–2001*. Collections are given in reverse chronological order, and there's an index of titles and first lines. Print is set off by lavish white space, letting the text breathe easily on the page.

Reverse chronology works well: Dunmore's poetry deepened with time, so the book makes a powerful start. She was always good, though, and in some ways her early work offers very different satisfactions to what came later.

Elements of what I most admire her for appear in the late 'September Rain', written as she neared her death: her empathy, her lack of self-centredness, her continuing joy in life and of course her technical skill and originality:

> There are three surfers out back.
> Now the rain's pulse is doubled, the wave
> Is not to be caught. Are they lost in the dark
>
> Do they know where the coast is combed with light
> Or is there only the swell, lifting
> Back to the beginning
>
> When they ran down the hill like children
> Through this rain, September rain,
> And the sea opened its breast to them?
>
> I lie and listen
> And the life in me stirs like a tide
> That knows when it must be gone.
>
> I am on the deep deep water
> Lightly held by one ankle
> Out of my depth, waiting.

In some ways such writing is very cinematic: we're given ideas in abrupt glimpses, like pictures in a piece of film showing fragments of movement and light flashing against darkness, with jump cuts between the surfers and the speaker who lies picturing them. Caught in snatches, images leap across boundaries between literal and metaphorical statement, fact and fantasy, without settling into one category or another. It's more musing and inward than cinema can be, though; thinking of the surfers, Dunmore slides in and out of their minds, at one moment imagining things from their point of view, the next not knowing what they know. In a sense we're inside her mind, going with the flow of her thoughts, but she presents her own situation with reticence and remarkable objectivity.

'September Rain' has great rhythmical beauty. In a few poems Dunmore makes something like a virtuoso display of her skill in what Eliot called the 'auditory imagination', as she does in this stanza from 'Odysseus to Elpenor':

> Tell me how you came here
> Fleeing like a cloud shadow
> Over restless water –

More often, especially later, she uses such skill unobtrusively, downplaying lyrical, musical elements in favour of a spare, neutral approach, so that we're taken by surprise by the force of what's said when it suddenly comes home. The widely admired 'The Malarkey' is an obvious example.

In contrast, the writing in Dunmore's first two volumes brings breathless intensity to almost everything she writes about. Though pleasurable in short doses, such richness can drown broader pictures in their own details and stifle distinctions under a glaze of exquisite style. The new poems in the 1991 selection *Short Days, Long Nights* seem to be the point of transition to a more varied approach, presenting banal and mundane realities in blunt language, letting in the rougher cadences of speech, creating dynamic interactions between different ways of framing and feeling. An assured mixing of textures and registers seems to me essential to the power of the later work. This involves both subtle transitions which I could only illustrate by lengthy quotation, and strong, simple contrasts, as in 'The Place of Ordinary Souls', in which there's a bus to Hades whose 'passengers peel their thighs / from hot vinyl' while 'Swift-heeled Achilles strides / Through the fields of asphodel'. Either way, the ordinary in its essential wonder comes to seem more and more Dunmore's subject, however diversely and extraordinarily expressed. The idea that this is the only life recurs. As such, it is in itself a cherishable miracle. One of her last poems, 'My life's stem was cut' speaks with radiant simplicity at once as a cut flower and as a dying woman grateful for human kindness. In every word, perhaps through the gentleness of the rhythms, the perfectly ordinary seems bathed in a sacramental glow and art itself almost seems to disappear in the sureness of its own achievement.

Instructions Not Included

James Longenbach, *How Poems Get Made* (Norton) $15.95

Reviewed by MATTHEW VALADES

Poet and critic James Longenbach has been an essential voice in the study of poetic craft for decades. Formerly a critic for the *New York Times*, Longenbach's career has cut a path from writing about poetry primarily for an audience of scholars and poets to a more general readership. His most recent prior work of criticism, *The Virtues of Poetry* (2013), published by Graywolf Press, defines and examines twelve principles of poetic achievement with reflective, fast-shifting essays that include a fair amount of biography. In *Virtues*, Longenbach frames his insights with concepts ranging from playful to lofty in chapters such as 'The Various Light', 'Writing Badly', and 'Infinitude'. His latest book, *How Poems Get Made*, focuses instead on 'the most fundamental elements' of English-language poetry. Though at first glance the book's carpentry-like title might lead someone to think this is a manual for understanding how they too can write poems, it is in fact a tightly constructed guide to how poems become poetry – that is, to becoming a better reader.

The structure of the book is deceptively simple. Like many other guides to English-language poetry, each chapter focuses on a feature of language often used in poems. These range from familiar headings like 'Diction', 'Rhythm' and 'Syntax' to more unusual ones like 'Echo', 'Song' and 'Prose'. Close readings of poems written any time from 'Cædmon's Hymn' to the present comprise each chapter, with most selections taken from canonical Renaissance, Romantic and Modernist poets. Complexity arises from the interaction between chapters, with certain poems returning for comparison and an argument about what gives them life accumulating as the book develops. Longenbach's central idea is that master poets use the 'interplay' of unique features within their medium, in this case modern English, to create poems that can surprise us by capturing a 'linguistic act of becoming', an event created anew each time it is read.

For example, in an early chapter on diction, Longenbach focuses on word roots, how poets have used the shifts between Anglo-Saxon and Latinate words to create certain effects to which English, as a hybrid language, is well suited. When the hard-thumping plainness of the former collides with the 'officious' and sometimes 'magical' quality of the latter, a feeling of discovery can be created, a discovery that we experience as poetry. He draws an example from Yeats' 'The Tower':

> That, being dead, we rise,
> Dream and so create
> Translunar paradise.

The difference in sound between the simple 'being dead, we rise' and the wispy 'Translunar paradise' tickles the ear. Such effects create skillful shifts between registers that allow readers to, as Longenbach writes, 'feel we're grappling with more than one language at once, as if the act of writing in English were already an act of translation.'

The notion of interplay is applied to different elements of language in each chapter, giving the book a connective line of argument. A confident poet, the author is also able to play with alternative possibilities, such as writing out passages backwards or with different word choices, to illustrate how certain decisions affect a poem. His prose remains precise and inviting throughout. Like many good artists, Longenbach makes it look easy, revealing his insights in a fluid and non-repetitive way, even in the chapter on repetition.

Though I find the book's critical method of close reading and attention to language refreshing, its aesthetic commitment admirable, there does seem to be an overemphasis on literary devices at the expense of other ways to understand poems. Longenbach addresses poetry's relationship to the world in passing, writing that a poem is 'a transaction between the mind and the world that is played out in the material reality of the medium', a sound point. Though this topic also gets a paragraph in the 'Image' chapter, the book could have been enhanced by more attention to how poems relate to their subject matter and contexts.. If the transactions between poems and the world are framed only by the devices associated with traditional lyric poetry, poems of history, social witness or identity may be incompletely understood or just left out. Consistent with this, Jean Toomer is the sole writer of colour cited in the book, even among the contemporary selections. Despite these limitations, *How Poems Get Made* will be valuable for students of poetry and experienced poetry readers who would like a fresh tour of familiar territory from one of the most insightful poet-critics currently writing.

Wry Reading

Stefan Collini, *The Nostalgic Imagination: History in English Criticism* (Oxford) £25

Reviewed by TONY ROBERTS

'Literary critics are always, by default, second-hand historians,' Stefan Collini claims in his new book, *The Nostalgic Imagination*, and then goes on to illustrate this in forensic detail. His latest welcome examination of twentieth century British intellectual history is an amplification of the Ford Lectures delivered at Oxford in 2017. In these he argues that between T.S. Eliot's *The Sacred Wood* (1921) and Raymond Williams's *The Long Revolution* (1961), while academic history turned to specialisation, literary (and cultural) criticism took over some of its old territory in the national consciousness. Highly influential and generally unchallenged literary critics like T.S. Eliot, F.R. Leavis, William Empson and Raymond Williams contributed to both literary history and general history, without the necessary credentials in the latter.

Collini first dismisses one of 'the foundation myths' of literary studies, which argued that during 'The Age of

Criticism' these critics prioritised the text while denying the historical dimension of literature. He shows they were in fact concerned with a radical re-examination of history and 'played a powerful part in diffusing an understanding of a contemporary cultural identity that was closely tied to an account of the national past'. The problem was that they were reacting to old historical assumptions (largely the 'Whig' narrative of political and moral progress): 'To a surprising extent, some of the most radical critiques of "mass society" or "commercialism" in the middle decades of the twentieth century rested indirectly on pictures of the past drawn from such "authorities" as G.M. Trevelyan and J.L. and Barbara Hammond or even J. A. Froude and Leslie Stephen.'

Like Caesar, T.S. Eliot bestrode this narrow world like a colossus. Collini explores the master's unsupported comments on history and their amazing, evolutionary afterlife. Perhaps Eliot's most stunning assertion was of the 'dissociation of sensibility', which he described as 'something which had happened to the mind of England' between the seventeenth and nineteenth centuries. By his own repetition this 'sweeping yet offhand claim [came] to be treated as a serious contribution to the understanding of history'. (Witness Basil Willey and L.C. Knights, through whose work the ripple effect of Eliot's self-serving phrase entered the area of religious belief and the economic field).

While Collini is sympathetic to Eliot's position with respect to the boundaries between disciplines, he leaves the reader in no doubt as to the latter's irresponsibility in proposing large historical generalisations, only to retreat without modifying them, on the grounds of 'not trespassing on historians' territory'. To Eliot and company all was in decline from the seventeenth century onward, especially in the Victorian period. As Chris Baldick pointed out, in *Criticism and Literary Theory 1890 to the Present* (1996), Eliot's polemics further served as a rejection of the Victorian absorption with author rather than text (which had serious implications for criticism in England and America) and, in the wider field of British history, with its assumption of progress.

The Cambridge teacher and 'Scrutiny' editor F.R. Leavis, the other massively influential critic in England at the time, acknowledged himself greatly in Eliot's debt. Yet according to Collini he had 'carried a set of historical assumptions over from his doctoral work in the early 1920s', including a belief in a thriving eighteenth century reading public which the contemporary world could not match. In contrast to Eliot's selective targets however, 'Leavis has a more continuous historical story in mind'.

Another chapter asks whether William Empson was actually ahistorical, and of course he was not. I opened my copy of *Seven Types of Ambiguity* (1930) first and hit upon the same passage as Collini, where Empson quotes Shakespeare's Sonnet 73 ('Bare ruined choirs, where late the sweet birds sang') discussing its appropriateness, in his words, 'for various sociological and historical reasons (the protestant destruction of monasteries; fear of puritanism)'. Empson distanced himself from Eliot's neo-Christian atmosphere and Leavis's declinist position. Collini sees *Some Versions of the Pastoral* (1935) as a 'kind of meditation on aspects of English history' and his third major work, *The Structure of Complex Words* (1951), as 'informal intellectual history'. While Empson's historical assumptions often take the form of *obiter dicta* rather than direct statements, the implication is still that the critic's historical understanding relies on ageing texts.

The author discusses Raymond Williams's *Culture and Society 1780–1950* (1958) and *The Long Revolution* (1961), acknowledging that the former helped 'shape the wider public understanding of modern British intellectual history... an understanding that particularly flourished in the world of literary and related cultural studies'. Yet –as with the others –he is of the opinion that the history is defective. A key instance lies in Williams's decision to locate the birth of the concept of culture during the Industrial Revolution, earlier than is warranted by Collini's reading of the evidence. This afforded Williams the opportunity of co-opting more writers into a tradition – with Socialist implications. He also points to one post-war reading list Williams set for an adult class on 'Culture and Society' that included only three titles by professional historians among sixty-nine books.

Collini sees the Welsh author's work as another example of 'the misplaced intellectual imperialism' which had hampered literary criticism since Eliot.

The Nostalgic Imagination offers a second tier of 'misrepresentatives', which includes Q.D. Leavis, Richard Hoggart, the *Cambridge History of English Literature* and the ubiquitous, 'Scrutiny'-influenced *Pelican Guides* to English Literature. He also enters the 'Two Cultures' debate launched in 1959 by C.P. Snow's judgement that science and literature had become mutually mistrustful polarities. At the time Snow's friend J.H. Plumb observed that a negative view of material progress 'runs like dry rot through literary criticism'. We might wish to have heard more from Collini about historians' views on the criticism of the day though perhaps, as he suggests in one case, such work hardly registered on their thinking at the time.

Collini's book is leavened as always with sly humour. I particularly enjoyed his riff on Eliot's habit of announcing never written books. The author says in his postscript, 'I am, temperamentally or as a matter of intellectual style, more drawn to the microscope and to the fine grain of discrimination that it enables.' The reader has just had the benefit of this approach. I found *The Nostalgic Imagination* persuasive and relentlessly interesting. However, there is surely enough here to open up discussion in defence of one or another of its cast.

SOME CONTRIBUTORS

Andy Croft runs Smokestack Books. He also runs the T-junction international poetry festival in Middlesbrough and the Ripon poetry festival in North Yorkshire. He writes a monthly poetry column in the *Morning Star*. His most recent book is *Letters to Randall Swingler* (Shoestring). **Jodie Hollander**'s poems have appeared in *Poetry Review*, *The Yale Review*, *PN Review*, *The Dark Horse*, *Rialto*, *Australia's Best Poems of 2011*, and *Australia's Best Poems of 2015*. *My Dark Horses* is published with Liverpool University Press. **William Poulos** is a poet and commentator. Among his other projects, he is researching Alexander Pope's engagement with Latin poetry. **André Naffis-Sahely** is the author of *The Promised Land: Poems from Itinerant Life* (Penguin, 2017). His translations include over twenty titles of poetry, fiction and nonfiction. He is the poetry editor of *Ambit* magazine. **Michael Farrell** grew up in Bombala in the Snowy Monaro region of New South Wales, and now lives in Fitzroy, Melbourne. His latest book is *I Love Poetry* (Giramondo). **Sean O'Brien**'s ninth collection of poems, *Europa* (2018), was shortlisted for the T.S. Eliot Prize. His book-length poem *Hammersmith* is to be published by Picador in 2019. He is Professor of Creative Writing at Newcastle University. **Joe Carrick-Varty** won the 2018 New Poets Prize and his debut pamphlet *Somewhere Far* is published by The Poetry Business. **Jennifer Edgecombe** lives on the Kent coast. Her poems and reviews have appeared in *Ambit*, *Caught By the River*, *Lighthouse* and elsewhere. **Andrew Wynn Owen** is a fellow of All Souls College, Oxford. He received an Eric Gregory Award in 2015. *The Multiverse* was published by Carcanet in 2018. **Martin Caseley** is an essayist, poet and retired teacher now living in Norfolk. Previous pieces on Edward Thomas, Thom Gunn and Geoffrey Hill have recently appeared in *PN Review* and *Agenda*. **James Jennings** writes from Asia. After several years working at the Khmer Rouge war crimes tribunal in Cambodia, he currently lives in Myanmar. His first novel, *No Sell Dead, a Tale of Cambodia*, was published by Molecular Press in 2018. **Patrick Worsnip** is a former Reuters correspondent. His Carcanet Classics version of the poems of Propertius was the Poetry Book Society verse translation recommendation for Autumn 2018. **Christine Blackwell** is an American writer and editor from Detroit. She is a former editorial director for Houghton Mifflin Harcourt. **Edmund Prestwich** lives in Manchester and is the author of two collections, *Through the Window* with Rockingham Press and *Their Mountain Mother* with Hearing Eye. **Anthony Barnett**'s *Lithos* was reviewed in *PN Review* 239. Other books include *The Making of a Story*. He co-edits *Snow lit rev*. (www.abar.net). **Alastair Llewellyn-Smith** has been writing poems all his life, but only got going seriously at the beginning of 2016. He's had poems published in *Acumen* and *The London Magazine*. **Jonathan Farmer** is the author of *That Peculiar Affirmative: On the Social Life of Poems* and the poetry editor and editor-in-chief of *At Length*. **Tony Roberts**'s fifth collection, *The Noir American & Other Poems*, was published last summer. His second book of essays on poets and critics, *The Taste of My Mornings*, has just been published, both by Shoestring Press. **Matthew Valades** is a poet and MFA student at the University of North Carolina, Greensboro. His poems have been published in *Subtropics* and *Carolina Quarterly*. **Dan Burt** was born in South Philadelphia, read English at St John's College, Cambridge, and graduated from Yale Law School. He is a lawyer, businessman, writer and Honorary Fellow of St John's College, Cambridge. **Patrick Miles** has translated plays by Turgenev, Chekhov, Bulgakov and Vampilov for the Royal National Theatre and Abbey Theatre, Dublin. His latest book is *George Calderon: Edwardian Genius* (Sam & Sam, 2018). **Alex Wong**'s first collection, *Poems Without Irony*, was published by Carcanet in 2016. He has also edited the *Selected Verse of Swinburne* and the *Selected Essays of Walter Pater* for Carcanet Classics. **Charles Bernstein** is the author of *Near/Miss* (University of Chicago, 2018), *Pitch of Poetry* (Chicago, 2016) and *Recalculating* (Chicago, 2013). In 2019, he received the Bollingen Prize for American poetry.

COLOPHON

Editors
Michael Schmidt
Andrew Latimer

Editorial address
The Editors at the address on the right. Manuscripts cannot be returned unless accompanied by a stamped addressed envelope or international reply coupon.

Trade distributors
NBN International
10 Thornbury Road
Plymouth PL6 7PP, UK
orders@nbninternational.com

Design
Typeset by Andrew Latimer in Arnhem Pro

Represented by
Compass IPS Ltd
Great West House
Great West Road, Brentford
TW8 9DF, UK
sales@compass-ips.london

ISBN 978-1-78410-826-7
ISSN 0144-7076

Subscriptions (6 issues)
INDIVIDUALS (print and digital): £39.50; abroad £49
INSTITUTIONS (print only): £76; abroad £90
INSTITUTIONS (digital): subscriptions from Exact Editions (https://shop.exacteditions.com/gb/pn-review)
to: *PN Review*, Alliance House, 30 Cross Street, Manchester M2 7AQ, UK

Supported by

Supported using public funding by ARTS COUNCIL ENGLAND